THE
FRENCH POLYN...
Dive Guide

Text and photographs by
KURT AMSLER

Editing provided by
Rodale's Scuba Diving

ABBEVILLE PRESS PUBLISHERS
New York London Paris

THE
FRENCH POLYNESIA
Dive Guide

Page 1. Crystalline blue waters border the beach of Manihi, an atoll in the Tuamotu Islands famous for its cultured pearls.

Pages 2–3. A diver uses his flashlight to illuminate the amazing fans of gorgonians on the underwater walls off the coast of Tahiti.

Page 4, top. A school of silvery mackerels swims through the waters of Tikapo at Nuku Hiva, in the Marquesas Islands.

Page 4, bottom. Lush vegetation borders the beach of Bora Bora in the Society Islands.

SOCIETY ISLANDS

MATAIVA

LEEWARD ISLANDS

TUPAI

MAUPITI

BORA BORA

MAKATE

TAHAA

HUAHINE

TETIAR

RAIATEA

MOOREA

MAIAO

TAHIT

MEHETI

WINDWARD ISLANDS

TUBAI ISLANDS

MARQUESAS ISLANDS

HATUATUA   ILE de SABLE

EIAO

MOTU ITI

NUKU HIVA   UA UKA

UA POU   FATU HUKU

HIVAOA   MOTANE

TAHUATA

FATU HIVA

BASIN
TIKI

TAKAREA

TAKAPOTO   PUKAPUKA

TIKEAU   TIKEI

RANGIROA   FANGATAU

ARUTUA   TOAU   KAUEHI

KAUKURA   TAKUME

KATIU   MAKEMO

FAKARAVA   TATAKOTO

ANAA   MARUTEA   PUKARUA

HARAIKI   HIKUERU   REAO

TAHANEA   RERITOU   VAHITHAI

     HAO

MAROKAU

NENGO NENGO

      PARAOA

MANUHANGI   PINAKI

AHUNUI

TUAMOTU
ISLANDS

DUKE OF GLOUCESTER
ISLANDS

GAMBIER
ISLANDS

PACIFIC OCEAN

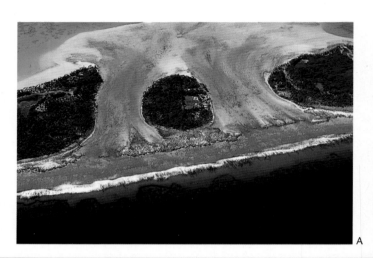

A. The land surface of the island of Maupiti, one of the Leeward Islands of the Society archipelago.

B. An extraordinary aerial view of the Bora Bora atoll, clearly of volcanic origin, in the Society archipelago.

The South Seas have always possessed an aura of unparalleled charm, the sweet scent of paradise, of stress-free living in close contact with nature and the ocean. Like green emeralds cast in the blue expanse of the Pacific, the 115 islands of French Polynesia are grouped into five archipelagoes—the Gambier,

A

B

Marquesas, Society, Tubuaï (Austral), and Tuamotu island groups—which together cover an area 1,860 miles (3,000 kilometers) long and 1,550 miles (2,500 kilometers) wide. French Polynesia is surely most symbolized by legendary Tahiti, the Island of Love, for centuries renowned as the "new Cythera," a paradise on earth. The explorers who first discovered these islands—Louis-Antoine de Bougainville, James Cook, and Samuel Wallis—were enthralled by Tahiti, enthusiastically describing the charming landscape and the grace and beauty of the natives. Early travelers to these remote islands tell of magnificent territories untouched by feared tropical diseases and free of wild animals and parasites.

A long list of famous authors, including Herman Melville, Jack London, Robert Louis Stevenson, and W. Somerset Maugham, have sought inspiration in Tahiti, fascinating readers around the world with their exotic adventures. Paul Gauguin, who traveled here as an unknown artist, became world-famous for capturing the colors and the people of these islands on canvas.

The Hollywood production *Mutiny on the Bounty*, which attracted millions to cinemas the world over, brought the South Seas to the notice of the general public at the beginning of the 1960s. More recently, the opening of an international airport in Tahiti and the influx of film stars like Marlon Brando who have chosen to set up house on the islands marked the beginning of a tourist boom. The extraction of mother-of-pearl and the worldwide trade in black cultured pearls that can only be produced in these waters are also of considerable economic significance, although tourism remains the biggest source of income.

The population is nearly 78 percent Polynesian. Six percent is Asiatic, especially Chinese, while the remainder is made up of mixed races and Europeans. Almost three-fourths of the islands' approximately 200,000 residents live in Tahiti.

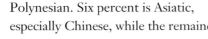

E. Nuku Hiva, the largest of the Marquesas Islands, is dominated by Mount Tako, rising 4,040 feet (1,224 meters) above sea level.

The History of Polynesia

The first settlers of the Pacific Islands came to the South Seas from South Asia some 3,300 years ago in huge dual-hulled canoes, fitted with palm-leaf sails and paddles. These Polynesians already had their own highly developed culture. They lived off fishing and agriculture, using bone, wood, and stone implements. The men were generally in charge of sowing food, fishing, and the construction of houses and boats, while the women looked after the fields, the harvest, and the preparation of meals. Polynesian life was marked by a large number of taboos, a word from the Polynesian *tapu*, "sacred and prohibited." For instance, it was taboo to harvest crops that were not sufficiently plentiful or to fish more than was necessary for current requirements.

The Polynesians were particularly skillful in the construction of seagoing vessels. Their canoes were not dug out as in other civilizations, but were built of planks held together with the resin of breadfruit trees. They dressed themselves with palm leaves, and made ornaments of the teeth of animals as well as fresh flowers. Both men and women were colorfully painted with palm oil and soot. Dancing and games were a passion of the islanders; the ancient Polynesian dances, to a music based on cylindrical drums and flutes, survive to this day. Tournaments of archery, javelin throwing, and wrestling were popular, as well as boat races. Soldiers used clubs, spears, and shields.

Although the history of Polynesia goes back 1,700 years, the first Europeans reached the islands only in the sixteenth century, when Ferdinand Magellan sailed past the Tuamotu Archipelago and Alvaro de Mendaña cast anchor in the Marquesas. On June 18, 1667, Captain Samuel Wallis, sailing on the *Dolphin*, reached Tahiti and immediately baptized it King George

A

II Island. A year later he was followed by the Frenchman Louis-Antoine de Bougainville. Since he had no means of knowing that Wallis had already been there, Bougainville claimed Tahiti in the name of the king of France.

The name Society Islands was given by Captain James Cook, who named these islands in honor of the Royal Society, which sent him there as an astronomer. In 1778 the famous *Bounty* stopped off at the island. After the mutiny, she was followed by the *Pandora,* in search of the mutineers in these waters.

The landing of the first English missionaries in 1791 led to inevitable power games and intrigues. Queen Pomare IV, who ruled for about half a century over Tahiti and Mooréa as well as part of the Tubuaï Islands and the Tuamotu Archipelago, was a devout Protestant and banned all French Catholic missionaries from her kingdom, especially Tahiti. Affronted, the French sent a heavily armed frigate to ensure their free access to the island. The queen's appeal for help to England fell on deaf ears, and brought France and England to the brink of war; though the Tahitians did all they could to avoid

B

this, French forts and war memorials still bear witness to this conflict.

When it became quite clear that no help was forthcoming from England, the queen and her people reluctantly agreed in 1847 to recognize the French protectorate. Despite assurances that not all the islands would be annexed, Queen Pomare was forced to watch silently as the greater part of Polynesia fell into French hands. After she died in 1877, her son and successor,

POLYNESIA,
OR
ISLANDS IN THE PACIFIC OCEAN

Pomare V, was more concerned with worldly pleasures than with the well-being of his people. In return for a life annuity, he in effect signed off the entire kingdom to France. In 1957 French Polynesia was declared a French overseas territory, and twenty-seven years later it acceded to domestic autonomy.

C

A. The explorer James Cook reached Tahiti in 1769.

B. This map from the late 1800s charts the islands of Polynesia and the Pacific Ocean.

C. A plate from an atlas of Cook's voyages shows the canoes in which the inhabitants of Tahiti welcomed the English vessel.

The Underwater World

Both divers and snorkelers in Polynesian waters enter a magical underwater world. The underwater landscape in the area is incredibly varied, with a combination of volcanic islands and coral atolls that allows for extraordinarily rich biodiversity. The warm Pacific waters surrounding the islands are full of nutrients that sustain a wide range of unique marine species.

The uniqueness of these species is already clear in invertebrates, such as strangely shaped starfish, sea urchins, and worms. The waters are teeming with all sorts of sea snails with multicolored shells and bizarre shapes, especially in the Marquesas Islands. Crustaceans such as crabs, lobsters, shrimps, and crawfish crawl over the corals with their sticklike legs or gather in large crowds before migrating. It is not rare to find up to twenty of these armored creatures in the crevices and holes in the reef.

Polynesia's extraordinary underwater world is an explosion of color. In every direction, the eyes feast on a host of colors, often created by thousands of multicolored fish in huge, dense schools, which keep close to the rocks or coral reefs for protection. In general these fish are juveniles, just a few days or weeks old, and keep together in defense against predators. It is only when they are larger that they become independent. This juvenile

A

behavior is not however universal, for in no other waters have I seen such large schools of fish as in Polynesia.

I was especially struck by the red soldierfish that populate the reef walls in thousands in many parts of the Tuamotu Islands. The same goes for the yellow pennant fish, the blue-striped grunt, and the wide-eyed perch that in ordered rank-and-file formations seem to be suspended in the current. Typical in these waters are the butter-flyfish and the emperorfish, which only grow to about 8 to 12 inches (20 to 30 centimeters), but come in surprising lively hues.

While snorkeling or diving in shallow waters around the reef or the coral blocks anchored in sand, one is almost certain to encounter speckled butterflyfish (Chaetodon citrinellus) and royal angelfish (Pygoplites diacanthus). Two very special representatives of another family, the clown triggerfish (Balistoides conspicillum) and the black-bar triggerfish (Rhinecanthus aculeatus), hold center stage on the reef.

I could go on for several pages to describe the shapes, colors, and behav-ior of the wonderful exotic fish of Polynesia, even though they make up but a very small part of the life forms on and around the coral reefs.

While the lower marine animals and fish are fascinating for their form and color, other creatures are equally impressive in appearance. At each dive, one is sure to encounter groupers, for instance. These large predators hang around motionless above the reef or in holes as they wait for their prey, which they gulp up in a single quick move-ment of their huge jaws. Since groupers do not actually masticate their prey, instead of teeth they have short,

pointed serrations with which they hold it. Groupers grow to a respectable size; in areas frequented by divers they are as friendly and trusting as puppies and often follow divers. Incredibly, the largest of the grouper family, the so-called jewfish, grows up to 10 feet (3 meters) in length and can weigh over 600 pounds (several hundred kilograms). In theory a grouper of this size could easily gulp up a man whole!

The Napoleon (humphead) wrasse

A. Polynesian waters are home to dense schools of fish such as these striped snappers, close to the bottom at Tiki, near Mooréa, in the Society Islands.

C

B. A camera flash lights up the lively col-ors of these bigeyes, swimming close to the bottom with a diver.

C. The passes, washed by nutrient-rich cur-rents, are often fre-quented by longfin bannerfish. This pic-ture was taken at Bar-racuda Point, near Rangiroa, in the Tu-amotu Archipelago.

is another reef inhabitant that generally swims in small groups of various sizes. It owes its name to the hump on its forehead, which gives it the profile of a French general wearing his three-cornered hat.

The vast shallow sand beds of lagoons are the ideal breeding ground for odd-looking bottom-dwelling species. What at first glance seems an uninteresting underwater desert emerges as an oasis of life upon closer observation. The seabed is covered with flat flounders lying camouflaged on the sand. The white and copper-colored fire goby (*Nemateleotris magnifica*) float in couples over their sand holes and immediately dart back into their homes at the first sign of danger. Gobies (*Valenciennea* sp.) behave as timidly, and live in symbiosis with bulldozer crabs. Generally one can only see the eyes of the lizardfish (*Synodus variegatus*), since the rest of its body is buried in the sand. As the sandy seabed slopes into deeper waters, countless spotted garden eels (*Heteroconger hassi*) sway upright in the current among the dunes. These fish

A

B

always have one-fourth of their bodies buried in the sand. As the diver approaches, they disappear together under the sand in perfect synchrony.

The seas of Polynesia are also home to the forebears of the common vertebrate species. These sea creatures with cartilaginous skeletons have lived in these waters for several hundred million years, and include species like nurse sharks and rays, especially stingrays, which are especially numerous here. These creatures can reach a wingspan of 5 feet (1.5 meters) and have a long tail with a poisonous sting. Stingrays are generally completely harmless and only use their stings in self-defense. On several islands such as Bora Bora and Mooréa, they have become an attraction for tourists, who swim and dive with them.

Where the turquoise blue of the lagoon turns into a deep blue, inter-

A. Polynesia is also famous for its dense schools of fish. This school of jacks was photographed at Manta Point, in the Rangiroa Atoll in the Tuamotu Archipelago.

B. Sharks abound in Polynesian waters, especially along reefs skirting the lagoon. These gray sharks "park" in the waters around Shark Cave, in the Rangiroa Atoll.

C. Squirrelfish generally swim close to coral reefs, which offer protection from predators.

D. A manta swims in the blue deep, looking for plankton. Encounters with mantas are especially common around passes, where the current brings in nutrient-rich water.

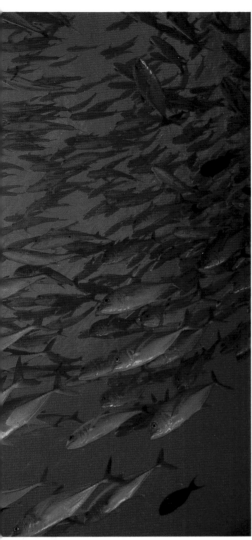

passes among the richest in sea life and the most spectacular for divers. Furthermore, these waters, populated above all by mackerels, are also home to dolphins and small whales. While sailing along the coasts of the islands or even in the open sea, one may well come across these intelligent marine mammals, who playfully follow boats, even at quite high speeds, entertaining passengers with their antics. Certain areas, for instance off the Marquesas

offspring eventually hatch on the beach. Following an as-yet-unknown synchrony, after a period of 40–60 days the young tortoises hatch at the same time. The wildly wriggling newborns rush directly to the water as fast as possible, in a race against death. Hundreds of frigate birds wait to feed on the easy prey, and a large number of newborn tortoises that escape the birds fall prey to beach crabs. Only half the hatched tortoises reach the sea

C

rupted only by the coral reef, the seabed falls off in abrupt drops that in many areas can be very deep. In Polynesia, these drop-offs into abysses are called tombants. It is here that one finds the huge creatures that inhabit the deep: manta rays and eagle rays, gray sharks, hammerhead sharks, and silvertip sharks, as well as schools of barracuda, tuna, and mackerel. With luck, one may also come across one of the largest fish in these waters—the whale shark, which is sometimes found in the large number of very deep canals that run through the lagoons to join the open sea. The very strong, constant current in these canals changes every six hours. For instance, millions of gallons of water pass to and fro through the Tiputa Pass with the tide. It is easy to imagine how much potential food is brought along with these currents, making these canals or

Islands are inhabited by melonhead whales that live in schools of up to three hundred. They do not seem to be afraid of man at all, and one can swim and dive with them. Not only small whales frequent these waters; every year entire families of humpback whales pass through the Tubuaï Islands.

The sandy shores and sandbanks of many islands are ideal breeding grounds for sea tortoises, who arduously lay their eggs in the sand here. On clear, moonlit nights it is fascinating to watch these reptiles emerge from the pitch-black waves like prehistoric monsters. Panting audibly, they haul their very heavy bodies, weighing tens of pounds, to the shore to complete their life cycle. Over several nights, each tortoise female deposits up to 150 eggs, which she places in different nests. While the mother swims in the open sea hundreds of miles away, her

safe and sound, and of these a large number fall prey to predator fish. Only one of five thousand newborns will reach adulthood and reproduce. This apparent wastefulness on the part of Mother Nature is, however, very necessary for the survival of this species, but nowadays this delicate balance is gravely threatened. Tortoises, exposed to increasing dangers, are still mercilessly hunted by man. Despite international laws for their protection, tortoise populations are dropping from year to year.

D

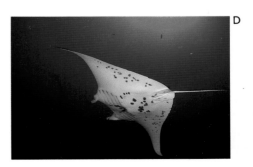

Diving in Polynesia

D iving in French Polynesia is professionally organized. All the islands open to tourists have well-equipped dive operations that conform to international standards. Some operators are members of the best union and apply uniform prices and guidelines. Each diver must have an internationally recognized diving certification (known as a *brevêt* in French). A log book is advisable to enable the dive guide or divemaster to get a better idea of the diver's practical experience. Generally, diving equipment is included in the price of the excursion. The basic equipment includes: the air tank, a regulator and pressure gauge, a BC (buoyancy compensator) with direct-feed inflator, and the necessary instruments—that is, a dive computer for independent diving when the diver's skill level warrants this. Generally, divers are accompanied by these dive-masters or dive guides, and can benefit from their experience to see many more fish and interesting underwater sites as well as feel more assured and safe.

All dive shops operate with boats. Operators located close to dive sites, such as at Rangiroa or Bora Bora, transport divers in large dinghies or Boston Whaler–type boats. Other operators use larger modern motor-boats or aluminum craft especially designed for divers. Those who want to sleep and eat on the ship while diving can book a live-aboard. The 60-foot (18-meter)-long luxury catamarans belonging to the Croisières Archipel company are recommended for cruises to the Tuamotu Archipelago or the Marquesas Islands.

Polynesian dive centers are committed to protecting the underwater environment. It is strictly prohibited to bring any living or dead sea creature, shell, or coral to the surface. Care must be taken in planning the dive so as not to damage the coral reef.

At this point, it is perhaps useful to outline a few general rules of conduct that diving enthusiasts ought to follow, to set an example to other tourists as well as because of purely ethical concerns. One should refrain from consuming products made from sea creatures, such as souvenirs made from tortoise shells, sea shells, or snail shells, or dishes cooked with shark meat, rays, morays, or even balloonfish. Restaurants serving shark-fin soup or shark steaks should also be avoided. Always remember that these fish were captured in the very places in which they so fascinate divers.

A. A group of divers approaches the boat that brought them to the dive site in the Rangiroa Atoll in the Tuamotu Archipelago.

B. Good lights and well-placed strobes bring out the lively colors of the underwater world.

C. A diver watches a solitary jack from a safe distance in the waters off Bora Bora, in the Society Islands.

D. Thanks to its crystal-clear waters, Polynesia offers the chance to take spectacular photos of the underwater landscape.

Underwater photography

Many amateur divers have found a completely new dimension in their hobby and holiday trips through underwater photography. A desire to capture on film the marvelous colors of the fish and coral of Polynesian waters comes almost naturally to most divers. Through the camera, the diver can observe things more closely, get a deeper insight into the behavior of sea creatures, and generally enjoy a more intense underwater experience.

Many amateur divers have become underwater photography enthusiasts, but still many divers shy away from taking the first step, influenced by the widespread idea that underwater photography is very difficult and that it is nearly impossible to take good color pictures under the sea.

This may have been true years ago, when very complicated cameras and equipment had to be used. Today, the market offers many modern and easy-to-use underwater cameras that produce high-quality pictures. The most widespread are amphibious cameras such as Motomarine and Nikonos, which are designed to be perfectly waterproof and therefore do not require further housings. In any case, modern automatic cameras designed for use on land can be encased in special housings for underwater use. As with all specialized sectors of diving activities, it is a good idea to take a course in underwater photography. Such courses are now offered in diving schools all over the world.

French Polynesia offers ample opportunity for underwater photography. The clarity of the water is one of the main factors in photo quality. At certain dive sites in Polynesia, water clarity differs with the seasons, but it is very rare to find conditions that make photography impossible.

Sunlight also plays a vital role in underwater photography. It is a mistake to think that the use of a flash can completely replace natural sunlight, which plays an especially crucial role in wide-angled photographs. Because of the layout of the seabed and the contours of the reef, pictures are best taken close to surface, at a depth of 15 to 70 feet (5 to 21 meters). As a general rule, sunlight, which abounds in Polynesia, easily penetrates to these depths, giving a beautiful blue background to colors captured by the flash.

The clear waters allow the use of normal-speed film. Best results are obtained using 100 ASA film such as Fuji Sensia or Kodak Elite, since they reproduce very good blues and shining reds.

As I pointed out earlier, an under-

D

B

C

water flash is a must for colorful pictures, since the density of the water filters sunlight, making the most colorful fish and coral come out a dull blue-green in photos in at a depth of just 10 to 12 feet (3 to 4 meters). The TTL flash almost always provides for well-lit photographs.

The photographic opportunities offered by French Polynesia are limit-less, representing an endless challenge for serious photographers. Underwater landscapes with divers or schools of fish just above the coral reefs are always spectacular. A wide-angle lens must be used for these shots. Best results are obtained by using a lens with a focal of 20 to 14 mm. Lenses with normal focal length require the photographer to be too far away from the subject to get the entire picture. In this case, the light rays that fall on the film to produce the picture have to travel very far through the water before reaching the lens, resulting in pictures without contrast in a dull blue-green background. Besides shortening the distance from which the picture must be taken, wide-angle or fish-eye lenses also provide great focal depth over the entire picture. A focal length of 20 to 28 mm is ideal for smaller subjects, such as divers, gor-gonians, soft corals, spotted garden eels, and small schools of fish. At between 2.5 and 5 feet (0.8–1.5 meters), the photographer can obtain sharp, con-trasty pictures with great color fidelity.

D

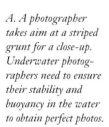

A. A photographer takes aim at a striped grunt for a close-up. Underwater photographers need to ensure their stability and buoyancy in the water to obtain perfect photos.

B. The crystalline waters of Polynesia and the lively colors of local fish afford ample opportunity for striking photographs.

C. The holes and crevices in reefs make for excellent photographic subjects, as in this picture of squirrelfish with their splendid red hues.

For single fish, sea anemones, sections of coral formations, smaller schools of fish, and gorgonians, the best focal length is 35 to 50 mm. With these lenses, focal depth is not very great, and therefore the photographer must be careful to use a lens setting of f/8 or f/11. Thus, the distance between the subject and the camera should be about 3 feet (1 meter) at most.

The fascinating world of close-up and zoom photography should not be neglected. Countless lower animals—colorful sea slugs and worms as well as shrimps and crabs—live on, in, and around coral formations. Details of soft corals, sea anemones, sponges, hagfishes, and gobies make ideal close-up subjects. Photographing these tiny subjects is easy with the right accessories—auxiliary lenses, intermediate rings, or zooms.

Special care must be taken to protect photographic equipment in the tropics and in salt water. After each dive, the camera must be not only washed but soaked in fresh potable water for about 10 minutes to eliminate sand particles and salt crystals from moveable parts and O-ring seals. To ensure that the camera and flash are perfectly waterproof, check the O-ring seal for

residue each time you change film, using your fingers. This also helps to pinpoint any damage.

After each diving holiday, soak all underwater photographic equipment 30 minutes in a bath of a spoonful of vinegar for each quart (liter) of water, which removes all salt corrosion from metal parts. Leave equipment to soak for another hour in potable water, dry all the parts, and grease the O-ring seals or, if they will not be used for some time, store them safely to maintain their shape.

Throughout Polynesia, the main supply voltage is 220V.

D, E. Large subjects, such as the sharks in the picture above and the Napoleon wrasse below, make wonderful photographs, especially against the deep blue of the water.

E

THE SOCIETY ISLANDS

LEEWARD ISLANDS

N

TUPAI

MAUPITI

White Valley ▼
Manta Dance ▼
Tupitipiti Point ▼
BORA BORA

Toahotu Pass ▼
TAHAA

Fa' a Miti ▼
Avapehi Pass ▼
HUAHINE

Tombant des Napoleons ▼
Wreck of the Norby ▼
RAIATEA

MAIAO

A

B

The Society Islands were discovered in 1779 by Captain James Cook, during an expedition aimed at collecting astronomical data. These volcanic islands, named for the British Royal Society, which financed Captain Cook's expedition, are now a major tourist attraction. The islands exposed to the trade winds are known as the Windward Islands, while the western islands are called the Leeward Islands. The Society Islands include Tahiti, Mooréa, Huahine, Raiatea, Tahaa, Bora Bora, and Maupiti. The two Windward Islands, Tahiti and Mooréa, have become world-famous thanks to the film *Mutiny on the Bounty*. The largest island of the archipelago is Tahiti; its capital is Papeete.

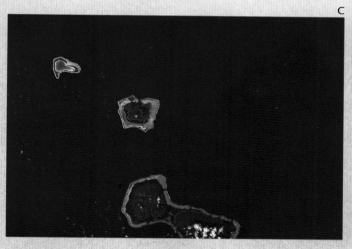

C

D

E

TETIAROA

Opunohu–Rose Garden

Taotoi ▼

Tiki ▼

Faille Pomare / Gorgone ▼

MOOREA

TAHITI

MEHETIA

W I N D W A R D   I S L A N D S

A. The island of Bora Bora, covered by luxuriant vegetation, and its splendid surrounding lagoon are dominated by the volcano Otemanu, which rises up to 2,399 feet (727 meters) above sea level.

B. Extraordinarily clear skies made this aerial view possible, showing the entire Tupai Atoll, part of the Leeward Islands in the Society Islands archipelago.

C. The Tupai, Bora Bora, and Raiatea atolls, seen from the space shuttle. This picture clearly shows the volcanic origins of the islands and the coral reefs that surround them.

D. This aerial photograph highlights the unique nature of the Polynesian atolls, focusing especially on the Maupiti Pass, the westernmost of the Society Islands.

E. The transparent waters of the lagoon of Tahiti are home to a wide variety of underwater life. Tahiti is the largest of the Society Islands.

The Island of Tahiti

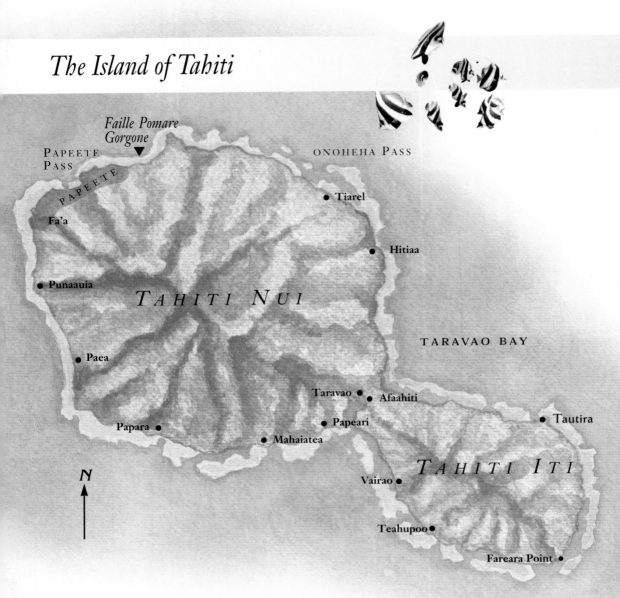

Faille Pomare
Gorgone

ONOHEHA PASS

PAPEETE
PASS

PAPEETE

Fa'a

Tiarel

Hitiaa

Punaauia

TAHITI NUI

Paea

TARAVAO BAY

Taravao • Afaahiti

Papeari

Papara

Tautira

Mahaiatea

TAHITI ITI

Vairao

N

Teahupoo

Fareara Point

B

A. This traditional fishing structure lies in the calm waters in the lagoon off Tahiti, which is very rich in fish.

B. The picture shows most of the Tahiti atoll, especially the northern area known as Tahiti Nui. In the foreground lies the largest city in French Polynesia, Papeete, with the runway of the Fa'a international airport. Given the high mountains, the island is often covered by clouds.

Legendary Tahiti, the largest of the Society Islands, is the gateway to eastern Polynesia. Nearly all visitors to Tahiti arrive at the Fa'a international airport, 3 miles (5 kilometers) from Papeete. Tahiti, which is formed by extinct volcanoes, accounts for almost a fourth of the dry land area of eastern Polynesia. The green peaks of Mount Orohena and Mount Aorai, which lie almost at the center of Tahiti Nui, rise respectively to 7,395 and 6,798 feet (2,241 and 2,060 meters) above sea level, while another 4,290-foot (1,300-meter)-high peak overlooks the other peninsula, Tahiti Iti. The vast majority of the inhabitants live in Papeete, the political and commercial capital of Polynesia, or along the coast.

A

It is worthwhile to spend at least one day or night on Tahiti, to experience its rhythm of life.

HISTORY

The history of the European discovery of Tahiti dates back to June 18, 1667, when Samuel Wallis, sailing on the *Dolphin*, reached the island and named it King George III Island after raising the British flag, the Union Jack. Unlike the inhabitants of the Tuamotu Islands, the inhabitants of Tahiti were well disposed to the foreigners and established a flourishing barter trade with them. Wallis was followed a year later by the Frenchman Louis-Antoine de Bougainville, who, not knowing that Wallis had already been there, promptly claimed Tahiti in the name of the king of France. The struggle over Tahiti and all of eastern Polynesia was to continue for over a century, until King Pomare V ceded the entire area to France.

DIVING

At present, there are several dive clubs and centers on Tahiti, which rely on customers who are mainly locals living on the island or others who wish to spend some time in the French Overseas Territory (Territoire Français d'Outre Mer), and those who dive for fun. A list of dive operators can be obtained at most hotels or at the Tahiti Tourist Office at Fare Manihini on the seafront. Most dive sites are on the northern coast going up to Venus Point, and continuing southward along the eastern coast.

C

D

FAILLE POMARE

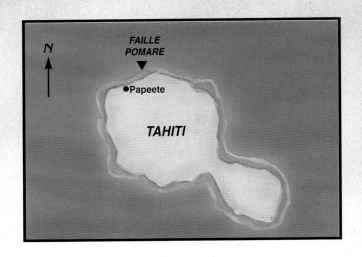

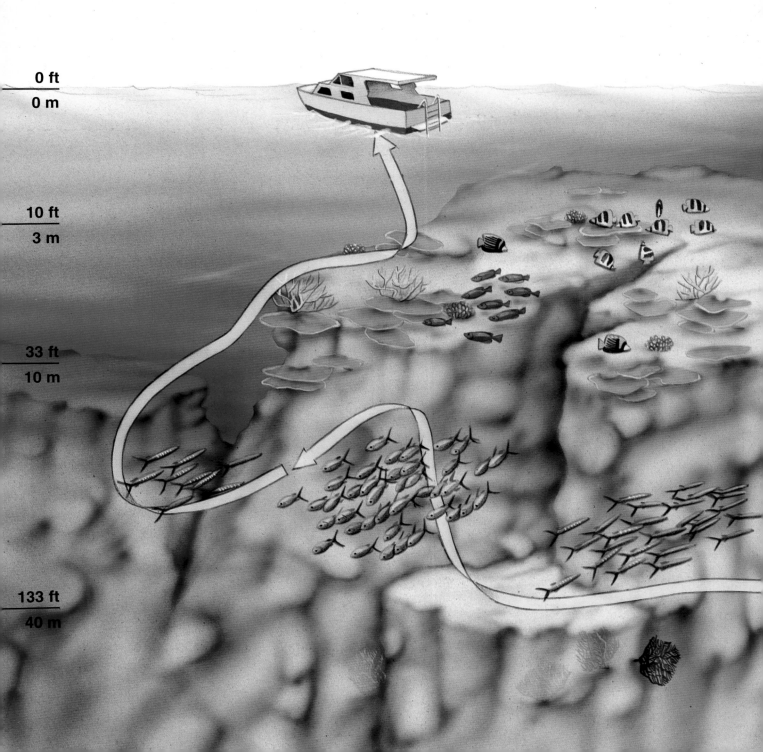

0 ft
0 m

10 ft
3 m

33 ft
10 m

133 ft
40 m

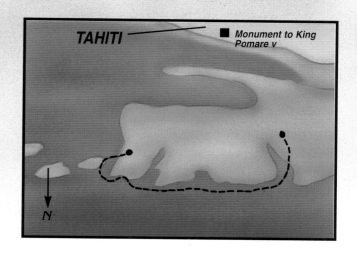

TAHITI

■ Monument to King Pomare v

N

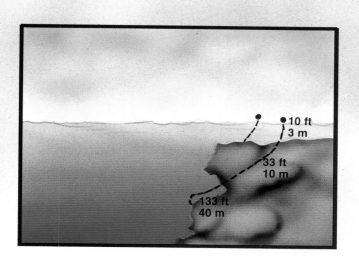

10 ft
3 m

33 ft
10 m

133 ft
40 m

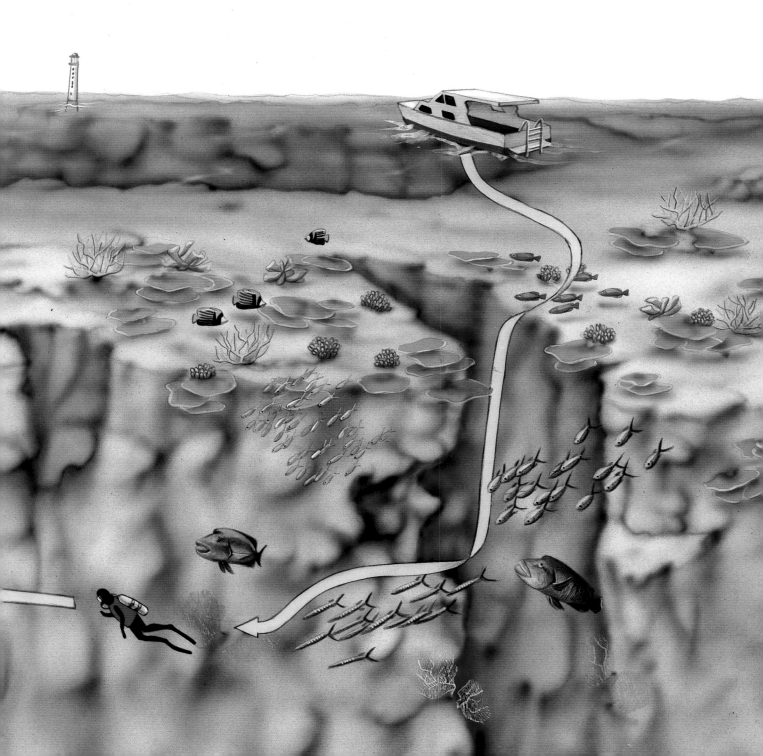

Faille Pomare lies off the north coast of Tahiti. Access is by boat from the Tahiti Yacht Club. The route first skirts the lagoon to lead through a canal (pass) to the open sea. The dive site lies to the west side of the pass.

The island is named for the monument dedicated to King Pomare V that stands on the coast. Since this king was more devoted to drinking and worldly pleasures than to the well-being of his subjects, his monument is crowned with a large bottle of liquor.

The dive site lies on the north side of a reef that rises from the seabed up to 10 feet (3 meters) below the surface. The reef falls almost vertically to the seabed at a depth of 1,320 feet (400 meters). Here, divers can explore both Faille and Faille Pomare. The choice of site depends largely on the direction of the current. From the top of the reef, located between 10 and 17 feet (3 and 5 meters) below the surface, the coral wall drops off perpendicularly, and, since the wall is full of projections, the underwater landscape is really spectacular. When the sea is calm, this site is suitable for all skill levels, since the depth can be adjusted to suit each individual diver. This site is, however, generally dived

B

C

A

A. The waters of Faille Pomare are inhabited by a wide variety of marine species. This picture shows butterflyfish swimming side by side with bigeyes.

B. In the foreground, the magnificent colors of the Napoleon wrasse, a rather peaceful fish, often encountered near Faille Pomare.

C. Coral formations often develop in bizarre shapes to capture the sunlight that filters through the water, as well as nutrients borne by currents.

D. The open sea off Faille Pomare is often frequented by dense shoals of silver-hued jacks.

E. Faille Pomare's uniquely shaped coral formations form the backdrop to a very lively reef population. The picture shows a shoal of squirrelfish that almost seem to pose for the photographer.

D

E

by experts who seek the thrill of following the reef face to a depth of over 130 feet (39 meters) so as to better enjoy the delights of the coral reef. However, regardless of depth, this site requires divers to strictly adhere to a set dive plan during the entire dive.

In calm conditions, the boat leaves the Yacht Club to head west toward the pass, home to a large school of dolphins that will almost invariably follow the boat, entertaining passengers with their spectacular acrobatic antics. The waters around Faille and Faille Pomare are inhabited by a large variety of members of the Chaetodontidae family (butterflyfish). Few dive sites are as rich in butterflyfish, emperor fish, surgeonfish and a wide range of other tropical species, all of which can be found close to the sunlit summit of the reef and in the waters immediately below.

Close to the surface above the reef, but also at greater depths, one will encounter Napoleon wrasse that are not afraid of divers, and sometimes follow diving parties for the entire duration of the dive. Schools of jacks, on the other hand, are more common in the open water, away from the reef. Although Tahiti is devoid of sandy beaches on which sea turtles lay their eggs, these wonderful, highly intelligent creatures are common in the waters around the island. Under overhangs and in the holes of the reef, one will find large schools of soldierfish. The emperor fish (*Lethrinus divaceus*), although quite rare in other parts of Polynesia, is commonly encountered here, foraging for food around the reef. The waters around this reef are also home to the tripletail, a species featuring great camouflage. These creatures adapt their shape and color to perfectly blend into their surroundings, and you will need the observant eye of a local dive guide to pinpoint them.

GORGONE

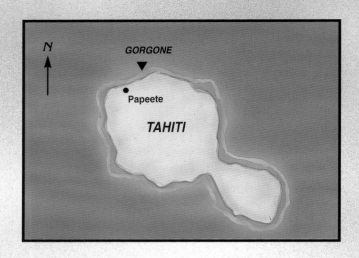

GORGONE

Papeete

TAHITI

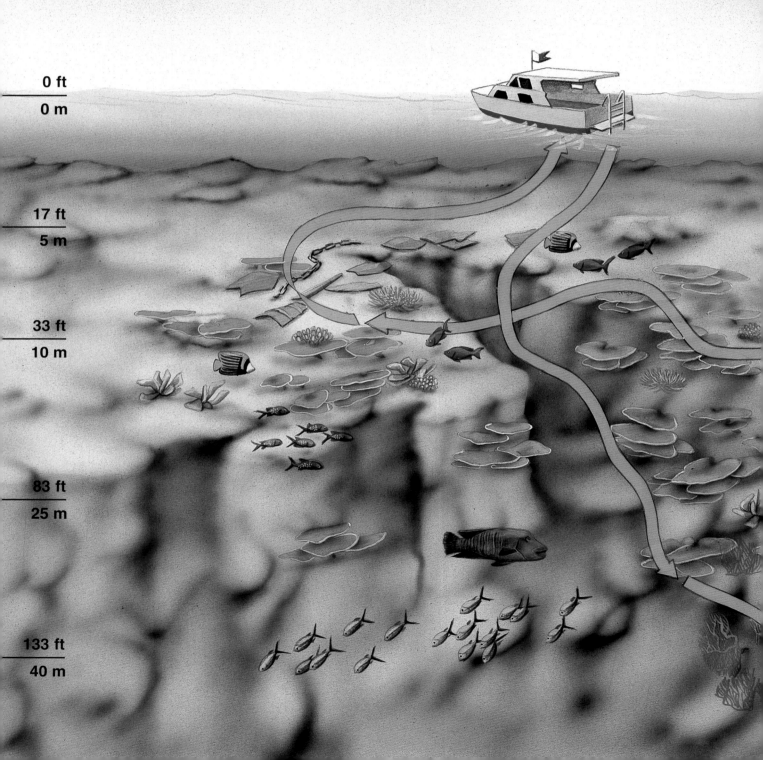

0 ft

0 m

17 ft

5 m

33 ft

10 m

83 ft

25 m

133 ft

40 m

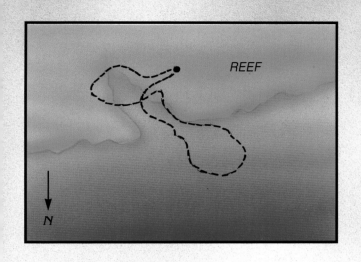

REEF

N

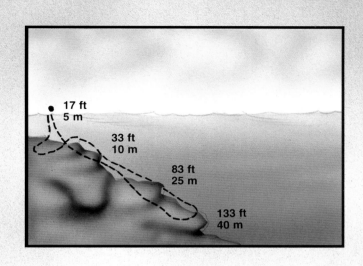

17 ft
5 m

33 ft
10 m

83 ft
25 m

133 ft
40 m

Like Faille and Faille Pomare, Gorgone is located off the north coast of Tahiti, at a distance of about half a nautical mile.

The underwater landscape at Gorgone is similar to that at Faille and Faille Pomare. The main difference is that the reef at Gorgone, cut by a deep canyon, drops off in steps for about

165 feet (50 meters) below the surface. The dive site derives its name from its marine vegetation, which is especially rich at the point where the coral reef drops off vertically toward the deep. The landscape features a splendid forest of large orange sea fans (gorgonians).

The boat drops anchor generally at the mouth of the canyon. By this open-

ing in the reef lies the wreck of a vessel.

Swimming around the canyon, which is well protected from the current, at about 82 feet (25 meters) one reaches the stepped slope, stretching toward the depths. This deep platform, a very exposed area of the reef, is often traversed by strong currents. Divers should therefore keep close to the reef and take advantage of the protection provided by coral projections. At a depth of about 130 feet (40 meters), the slope ends in a sort of balcony surrounded by a forest of sea fans that drops into the deep.

The drop-off covered by the sea fans should only be explored by expert

C. In the waters of Gorgone, about 1.5 miles north of Tahiti, divers will come across extra-or-dinary coral forma-tions.

D

E

divers. This does not mean that less experienced divers should avoid the site altogether: even in the canyon and along its steep walls divers will no doubt experience fascinating encounters against the breathtaking backdrop of one of the most interesting underwater landscapes in Polynesia.

The summit of the reef lies at 17 feet (5 meters) below the surface and is covered by lush coral vegetation that shelters a rich variety of marine life. The main highlight at Gorgone, however, is by far its rich mantle of sea fans. These soft corals are not as common in Polynesia as in the Red Sea or the Indian Ocean. They are totally absent in the Tuamotu Islands, for instance, and can be seen in other areas only in very specific conditions. The forest of sea fans at Gorgone, therefore, is a true rarity. Like all soft corals, sea fans feed on the plankton transported by the current and there-fore tend to favor exposed areas of reef as in this region. One must bear in mind that sea fans are not "builder" corals, and they have a flexible skele-ton. They shun sunlight, flourishing in the darker recesses of the reef, at depths of over 65 feet (20 meters). Sea fans, as their name suggests, look like huge yellow, orange, and sometimes red fans. These colors can however only be seen with the help of a flash-light or by using a flash on the camera.

Close observation of sea fans will reveal that their surface is covered by thousands of tiny tentacles. These are the tentacles of the coral polyps that capture their food, the plankton washed past by the current. At the slightest touch, all these tentacles simultaneously withdraw.

Apart from sea fans, Gorgone is blessed with an extraordinary variety of marine life. As at Faille and Faille Pomare, the top of the reef is a paradise for lovers of multicolored tropical fish species, such as the wide variety of triggerfish, which are generally quite rare. These waters are also home to larger species, such as Napoleon wrasse and certain amazing groupers. Gray sharks are often seen basking stationary in strong currents, seemingly in a state of suspended animation.

A. Gorgone owes its name to the large number of sea fans (gorgonians) that have settled on the reef here, which makes an ideal habitat.

B. Besides sea fans, in the crags and cracks of the reef at Gorgone di-vers will also encoun-ter a large number of exotic fish species, like this shy porcupinefish.

D. While sea fans are widespread throughout the tropics, they are quite rare in Polynesian waters, making Gorgone a unique site.

E. The reef at Gorgone is exposed to very strong ocean cur-rents; facing the open sea, you may encounter dense schools of pelagic species, like these silvery bar-racudas.

The Island of Mooréa

OPUNOHU BAY

▼ *Taotoi*

Opunobu–Rose Garden

COOK BAY

Papetoai ●

▼ *Tiki*

● Paopao

M O O R E A

VAIARE PASS

B

● Afareaitu

● Mount Tohiea

TERUAUPOU PASS

● Haapiti

MATAUAVA PASS

N

Tautira

AVARAPA PASS

Mooréa lies only 10 miles (16 kilometers) away from Tahiti and is clearly visible from Papeete. The heart-shaped island, about 7 miles (12 kilometers) wide from east to west and about 11 miles (18 kilometers) from north to south, offers marvelous sand beaches and lush vegetation as well as a splendid view of the large blue-green lagoon from its volcanic peaks. The Italian film director and producer Dino de Laurentiis shot the film *The Bounty* here.

The high mountains of Mooréa protect its northern and northwestern

A

sides, where the dive sites are located, from trade winds. The dryer climate and the beautiful landscape have led to a tourist boom, and a great many hotels have been built here.

A. The coastline of the Mooréa atoll features beaches bordered by the turquoise water of the lagoon.

B. As can be seen in this photograph, Mooréa is curiously heart-shaped.

C. The Mooréa reef is often frequented by gray sharks.

D. Passes at Mooréa allow water to flow into and out of the lagoon.

HISTORY

Mooréa was discovered in 1767 by Captain Samuel Wallis, who named it Duke of York Island. The first European visitors to Mooréa were scientists, botanists, and astronomers interested in observing the transit of the planet Venus. Captain James Cook also threw anchor off the island, in the bay of Opunohu, but never saw the place now known as Cook's Bay. Once again, the *Bounty* is linked to the history of Mooréa; King Pomare I conquered the island in 1792 with arms contributed by the ship's mutineers. When Queen Pomare II, who succeeded him, reconquered Tahiti, Mooréa lost strategic importance.

C

D

DIVING

Mooréa's diving area proper lies to the north and along part of the western coast. One of the most spectacular sites is undoubtedly Tiki, frequently not only by gray sharks but also by lemon sharks, which are not very common elsewhere. This site is at the northwestern end of the island, at about 4 miles (6 kilometers) from Bathy's Club, the dive center at the Beachcomber Hotel.

Diving on Mooréa is professionally organized, and is regulated in accordance with international and French Polynesian standards.

OPUNOHU - ROSE GARDEN

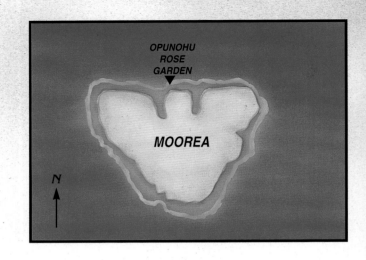

OPUNOHU
ROSE
GARDEN

MOOREA

N

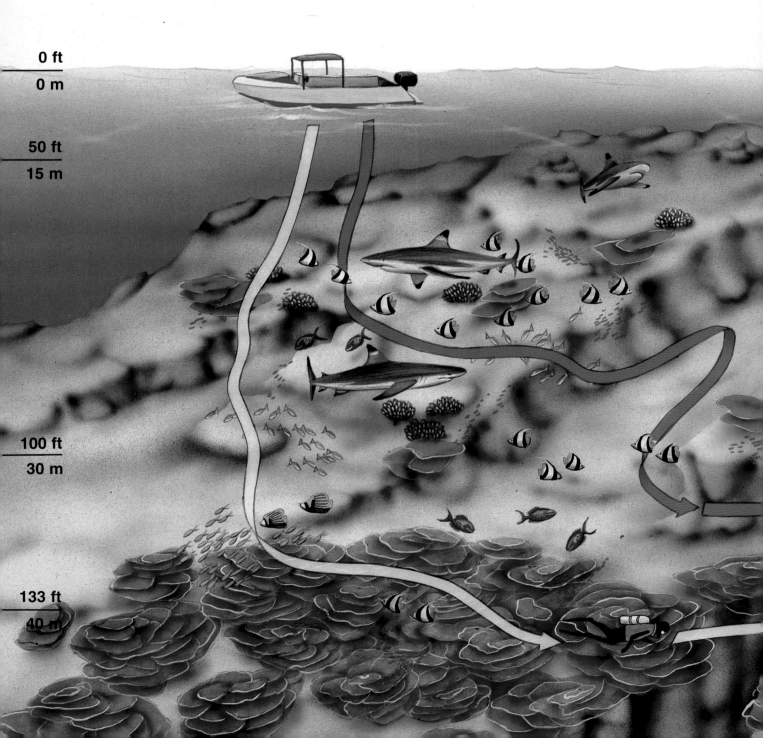

0 ft
0 m

50 ft
15 m

100 ft
30 m

133 ft
40 m

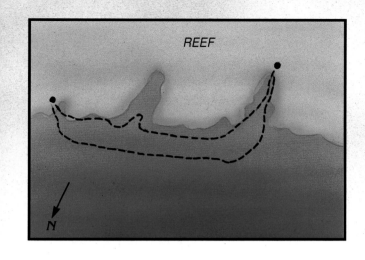

REEF

N

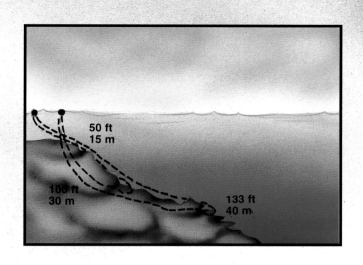

50 ft
15 m

100 ft
30 m

133 ft
40 m

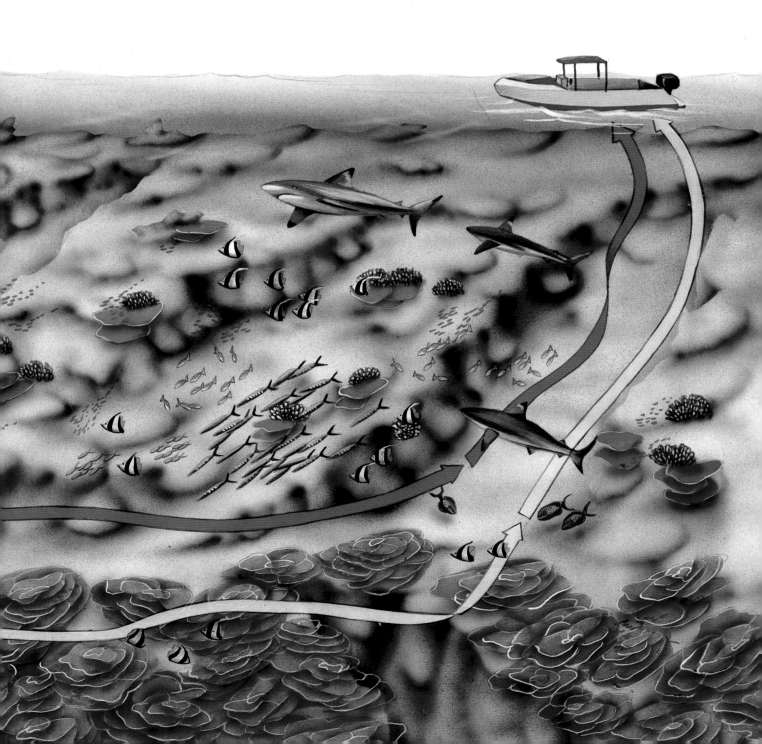

A. Opunohu is famous for its numerous blacktip sharks; divers can come across up to thirty sharks during a single dive. These sharks grow up to 6.5 feet (2 meters) in length.

B. Perhaps attracted by the divers who offer them food, the sharks come quite close to the divers without fear, although they seem to keep at a minimum safe distance.

Rose Garden lies almost at the center of the north of Mooréa, near Opunohu Bay. The position on the outer reef allows for crystal clear waters, large pelagic fish and an extraordinary reef totally covered by corals known as the Rose Garden. The coral-covered bottom, which descends steeply from a depth of 50 feet (15 meters), is actually the continuation of a coral platform that starts inside the lagoon. At a depth of about 100 feet (30 meters), the reef breaks its almost vertical drop to become a flat platform. Going down about 33 feet (10 meters) farther, one comes across a large expanse of montipore coral with branches that look like leaves. The area

A

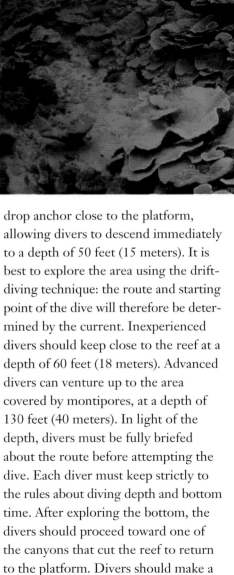

B

covered by the montipore is about 330 yards (100 meters) across and goes down to a depth of 200 feet (60 meters) below the surface.

Rose Garden should only be dived by expert divers. However, the dive can be planned to adapt the route to the diver's skill level. The boat should

drop anchor close to the platform, allowing divers to descend immediately to a depth of 50 feet (15 meters). It is best to explore the area using the drift-diving technique: the route and starting point of the dive will therefore be determined by the current. Inexperienced divers should keep close to the reef at a depth of 60 feet (18 meters). Advanced divers can venture up to the area covered by montipores, at a depth of 130 feet (40 meters). In light of the depth, divers must be fully briefed about the route before attempting the dive. Each diver must keep strictly to the rules about diving depth and bottom time. After exploring the bottom, the divers should proceed toward one of the canyons that cut the reef to return to the platform. Divers should make a safety or decompression stop in open

C. At a depth of about 130 meters (40 meters), the Opunohu reef is literally covered by large-leaved coral formations, a unique expanse of montipores that gives the area the name the Rose Garden. Given the depth, only highly experienced divers should venture here.

D. Blacktip sharks, among the most typical reef inhabitants, are easily identifiable by their light brown backs and white bellies. Furthermore, the tips of their fins are bordered in black. These sharks feed mainly on fish and squid.

These sharks, rather rare in deep water, can generally be found in the lagoon near the reef platform. Blacktip sharks are shy and generally avoid humans, unless attracted by the fish that divers try to feed them. Because of their yellowish coloring and large black-tipped fins, they are especially photogenic. Lemon sharks can also be found along the Opunohu Reef if one has a well-trained eye. This species, which can grow up to 10 feet (3 meters) long, generally swims close to the bottom and can be spotted only when it comes closer to the surface.

Divers who venture deeper, close to the expanse of montipore, will have very limited bottom time to admire the marine life on the reef, although they will be able to enjoy the spectacular Rose Garden and the breathtaking carousel of sharks. Novice divers can examine at leisure the extraordinary marine life in the crags and crevices of the coral reef, which is home to a wide variety of groupers. These large predators use their huge mouths to devour prey up to two-thirds of their own body weight. Divers lucky enough to see this will never forget the speed with which they capture their prey and swallow it whole with a single brisk movement of their jaws.

D

E. Three different types of groupers live on the Opunohu reef. The grouper in the picture is motionless, probably waiting for some unsuspecting prey, which it will swallow whole in a single gulp.

water, where there is a parachute that the divers can use.

Mooréa seems to be a paradise for blacktip sharks, which are especially numerous in Opunohu Bay, where divers are sure to come across groups of at least thirty fish, some of which reach a length of 6.5 feet (2 meters).

TAOTOI

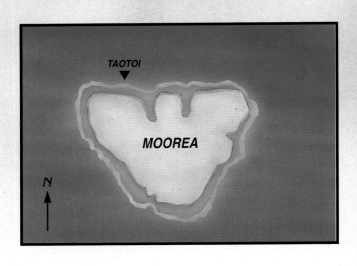

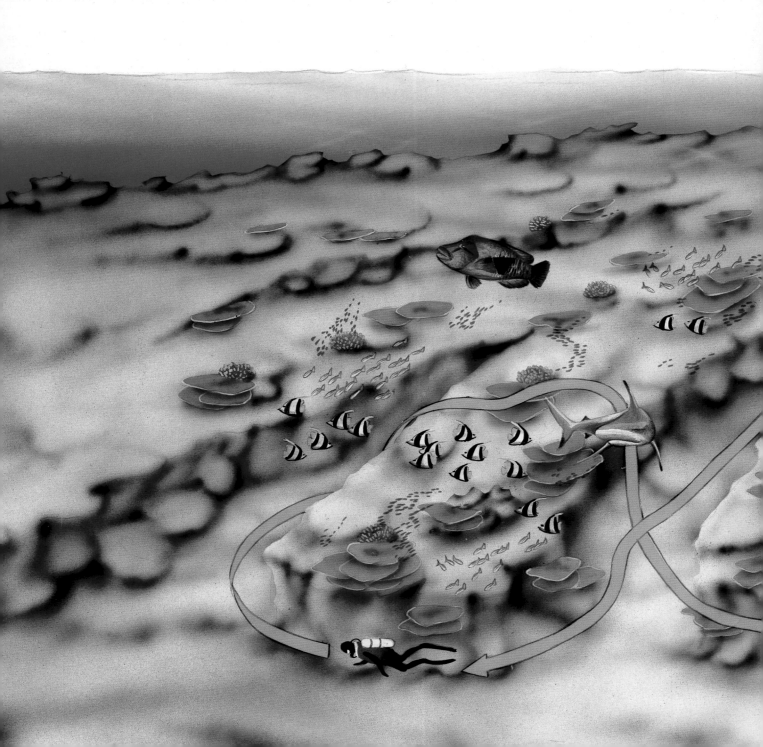

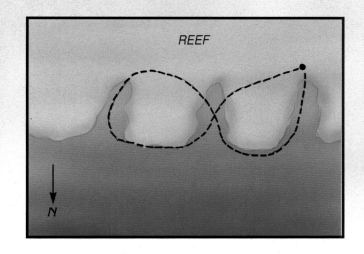

REEF

N

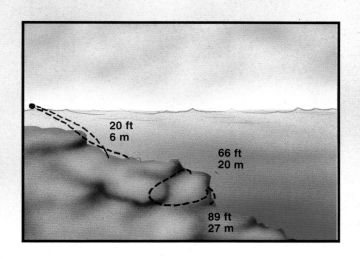

20 ft
6 m

66 ft
20 m

89 ft
27 m

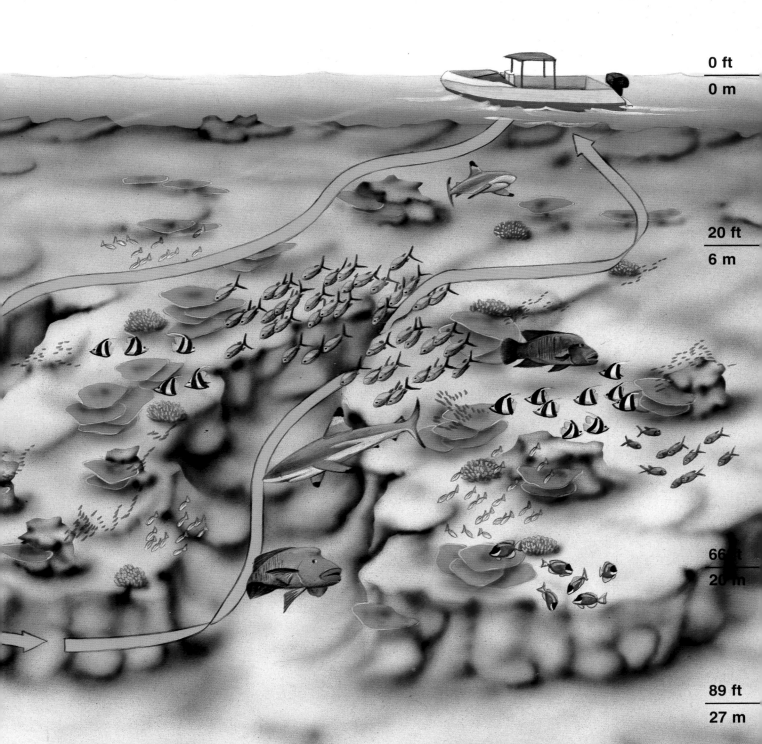

0 ft
0 m

20 ft
6 m

66 ft
20 m

89 ft
27 m

Taotoi lies on the north reef of Mooréa, just a ten-minute boat ride from the Bathy's Club. Here the reef slopes gently up to a depth of 130 feet (40 meters). The site features three huge canyons that cut through the reef, making this a truly memorable dive. Depending on diving skill, depths ranging from 20 to 130 feet (6 to

40 meters) can be selected.

Taotoi is well protected from currents, and diving is always possible, except when there is a strong north wind. The first buoy marking the dive site is anchored to the seabed at a depth of 20 feet (6 meters); the second, at 60 feet (18 meters), lies at the center of the first canyon. Divers using the second buoy should swim along the bottom to reach the foot of the reef, which is quite close to this point. Divers who choose to get into the water at the first buoy should swim in a north-

northwest direction across the reef to reach the second canyon.

Depending on the dive plan, divers can visit at least two, if not all three, canyons in a single dive. Even divers using a computer should strictly adhere to the dive plan, since the canyons can sometimes give rise to the so-called yo-yo effect. Divers should rise toward the surface only once during the dive, after having passed the summit of the reef. The rest of the dive should be continued at a depth of 65 feet (20 meters).

Although not in the same numbers as at Tiki, blacktip sharks can also be found at Taotoi. Another inhabitant of these waters is the Napoleon wrasse, which generally swim about in schools made up of adult fish that can reach a length of over 3 feet (1 meter), accompanying several juveniles. Although they stay at a safe distance, Napoleon wrasse tend to follow dive groups throughout an entire dive. These wrasses, which can grow to over 200 pounds (approximately 100 kilograms) in weight, are found throughout the tropics. The Napoleon wrasse, which owes its name to the prominent growth on its head, reminiscent of the profile of the emperor Napoleon, has strong teeth and feeds mainly on invertebrates, which it often hunts in areas of dead coral.

In the crevices of the reef at Taotoi, divers will find numerous moray eels, which often swim out of their holes in couples. This species has an elongated body, without pelvic fins. Moray eels are nocturnal predators; they leave their dens in the evening hours to hunt for prey, generally small fish and crabs. Their eyesight is not good, but it is amply compensated for by their highly developed sense of smell, especially useful for hunting at night. Since they must constantly filter water through their gills, moray eels continuously open and close their large mouths, showing their sharp teeth—a habit that may make them seem aggressive at first glance.

F

G

A. The boat taking divers to the Taotoi dive site.

B. The reef of Taotoi is often visited by sharks in search of prey. Divers attract sharks as well, by offering them fish.

C. Air reserves and bottom time permitting, it is well worth taking a little time to explore the reef, with its extraordinary variety of marine life. This grouper seems to inquisitively observe the photographer.

D. Napoleon wrasse swim in a family school.

E. This diver seems to be following a school of butterflyfish.

F. This picture was only possible thanks to the crystal-clear water: a squirrelfish accompanied by a small group of snapper.

G. Moray eels have made their dens in the cracks and crevices of the reef at Taotoi. They sometimes swim out of their homes in couples.

TIKI

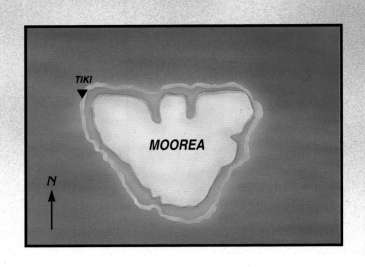

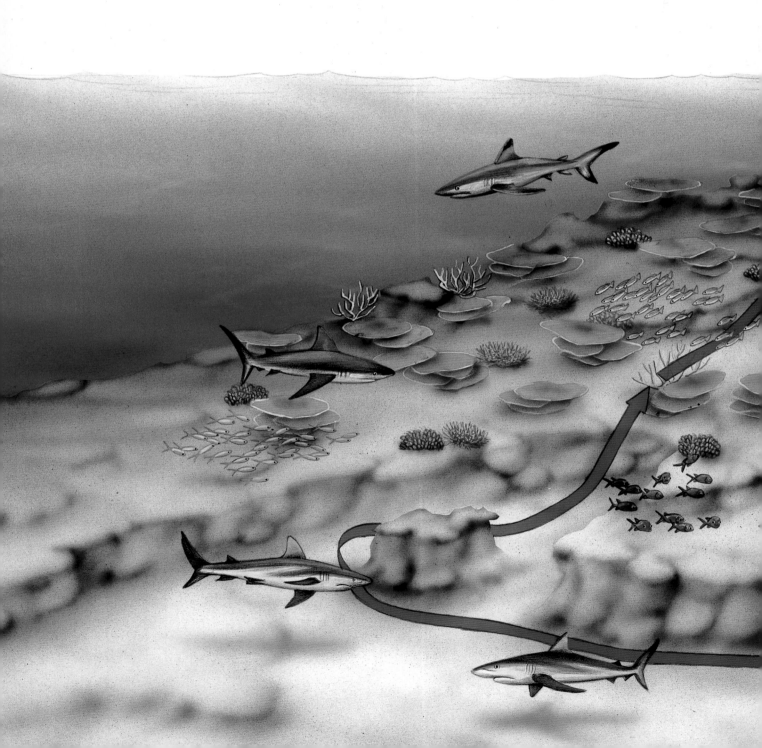

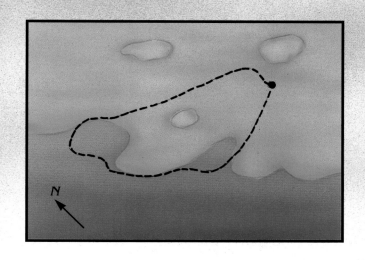

N

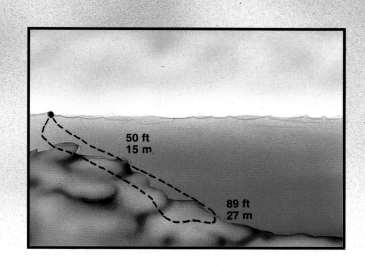

50 ft
15 m

89 ft
27 m

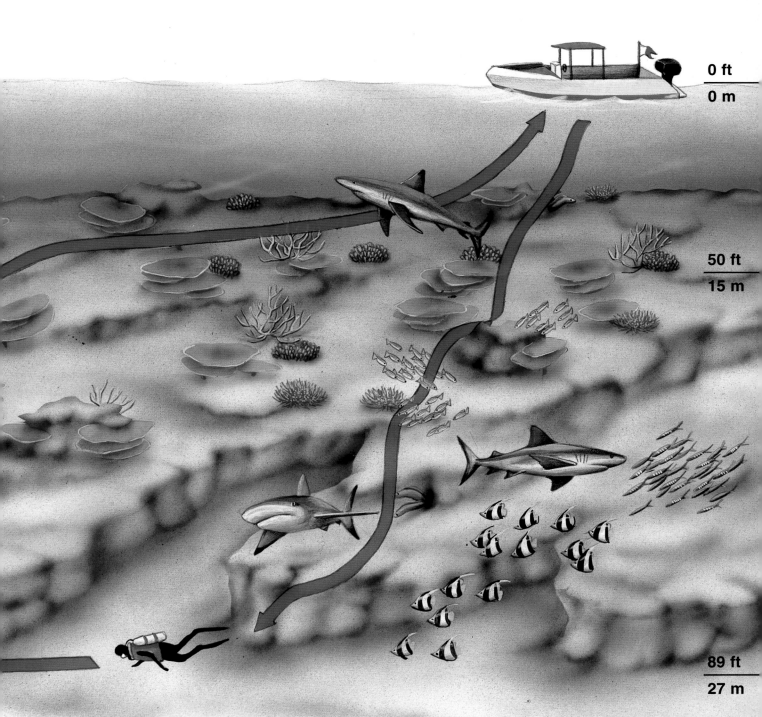

0 ft
0 m

50 ft
15 m

89 ft
27 m

Tiki lies off the northwestern tip of Mooréa, and diving is always possible here except in the case of strong west winds. Sharks are the main attraction at Tiki, where they have been accustomed to being fed by divers over the past few years, and therefore find the dive site a safe haven. The reef surrounding Mooréa slopes gently at Tiki from just a few feet below the surface up to a platform at the depth of about 100 feet (30 meters). Sharks are fed at a depth of 90 feet (27 meters) at a point where the reef curves inward to form a sort of creek.

Tiki is on the outer reef and requires a fair amount of diving experience. All dive groups in Polynesia must be accom-

A

panied by a trained dive guide, and all divers must be fully briefed on the dive plan before getting into the water.

The boat will generally be attached at a buoy anchored to the seabed at a depth of 50 feet (15 meters). Divers should get into the water at the buoy and descend to the bottom along the buoy line, then turn westward to swim over the reef that slopes gently to reach a canyon at a depth of about 100 feet (30 meters). Divers should then swim northward along the canyon to once again reach the main reef, which forms a small cut. At this point a large number of fish and small sharks will surround the divers, waiting to be fed by one of the dive guides, who carries the "bait"

B

in a bag. The little cut seems to become a real arena as the divemaster takes out the bait from the bag and the larger sharks are attracted from the deep to take part in the feast. This is the time to check air reserves and calculate remaining bottom time: in general, under normal conditions, the dive party can enjoy the show for about 15 to 20 minutes before returning to the boat.

The process of training wild sharks to take food from divers' hands is not very difficult. Basically a certain amount of food is thrown into the water at the same point everyday for several months. The sharks soon learn to recognize the spot where they find abundant food on a regular basis, and after some time a

A. A inquisitive moray eel peeks out of its den.

B. Tiki is famous for its large population of sharks. While blacktip sharks are the most numerous here, one also finds gray and lemon sharks. In these waters, fish attracted by the food brought to them by divemasters swim fearlessly right up to the divers.

C. The blacktip shark in this picture seems to be in a "food frenzy" unleashed by the food brought to the site by dive guides.

D. Lemon sharks are rather rare in Polynesian waters, although at Tiki they are quite commonly seen swimming close to the reef.

few sharks will set up home close to the feeding area. At this point, the dive guides can switch from offering the food using buoys to feeding the sharks directly with their hands. As an ever-increasing number of divers fondly recount tales of their shark-feeding experiences, the species is quickly losing its traditional reputation as a ferocious killer of the deep. Shark feeding has also resulted in a tourism boom that injects precious foreign exchange into the Polynesian economy. A healthy shark is far better off than a dead shark or a shark fished for its fins. As populations become increasingly sensitized to marine environmental issues, governments have been pressured into banning shark fishing.

Three distinct shark species can be found at Tiki. Blacktip sharks are found in shallower waters, sometimes immediately below the boat when the divers enter the water, in schools that can include up to thirty members. On good days, ten to fifteen gray sharks

can be seen swimming around the creek of the reef. Furthermore, Mooréa is perhaps the only place in the world where divers can get a close view of lemon sharks. Growing up 10 feet (3 meters) in length, these creatures have powerful bodies and an imposing silhouette. Their slightly parted mouths show a first row of sharp, long teeth. Unlike gray sharks, lemon sharks never swim in the open sea, but stay just under the surface—a real challenge to under-water photographers, who struggle to capture their beauty against the glittering blue background of the sunlit water.

Tiki features a rich variety of marine life. Apart from typical reef creatures, these waters are also home to groupers, which are generally black with white spots. When the diving guide opens the bag to feed the fish, he will generally be swamped by a crowd of large jacks.

Furthermore, on the reef platform, just a few meters below the buoy, lies a coral formation that is home to a large number of moray eels.

The Island of Huahine

Maeva

HUAHINE NUI

MOTU VAVARA

Fare

Avapehi Pass

AVAPEHI PASS

Fiti

MOTU MURIMAORA

MAROE BAY

Maroe

Tefarerii

N

HUAHINE ITI

MAHUTI BAY

Haapu

Parea

BOURAINE BAY

MOTU ARAARA

AVEA BAY

A. Huahine Nui and Huahine Iti, surrounded by the same lagoon and covered with lush vegetation.

B. This aerial view shows the peculiar shape of the Huahine atoll. The motus, the islets around the coral ring that encloses the lagoon, are cultivated, while the steeper slopes of the volcanic island are uninhabited. The runway of the airport that links Huahine to nearby Tahiti can be seen to the right.

Huahine lies 105 miles (170 kilometers) west of Tahiti. If approached by air from the southwest, the surrounding coral reef seems heart-shaped, with the two islands of Huahine Nui and Huahine Iti almost symmetrically placed at its center. Together with the coral barrier that surrounds the lagoon, the islands have a surface area of 9 by 11 miles (14 by 18 kilometers).

The airport is only 3 miles (4 kilometers) north of the village of Fare, and the island can also be reached by ferry from Papeete. In good weather, the boat journey can be a thrilling experience. Huahine boasts a diverse landscape and beautiful beaches, and

C. The landscape of Huahine is varied, with sandy beaches interrupted by steep, rocky coasts. The high waves in certain areas attract surf lovers.

D. The emerald green waters of the lagoon of Huahine are renewed every day by an inflow through the five passes of the atoll.

C

the high waves left and right of Fare Pass make the island excellent for surfing.

HISTORY

Researchers believe that the islands were already settled 1,300 years ago. Even if the Dutchman Roggeveen, who discovered Bora Bora and Maupiti, sailed by these islands, it was once again Captain James Cook who grouped them with the Society Islands. During the nineteenth century American whalers came here to spend a few pleasant months away from the Antarctic winter. English missionaries have been here since 1809, accounting for the fact that over 80 percent of the population of the Leeward Islands is Protestant.

DIVING

The Huahine atoll features five passes that link the lagoon to the open sea. The dive sites presented here are on the western side of the island. Naturally, other canals and important sites on the outer reef provide for spectacular dives.

D

FA' A MITI

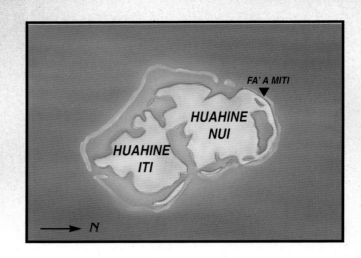

HUAHINE NUI

HUAHINE ITI

FA' A MITI

N

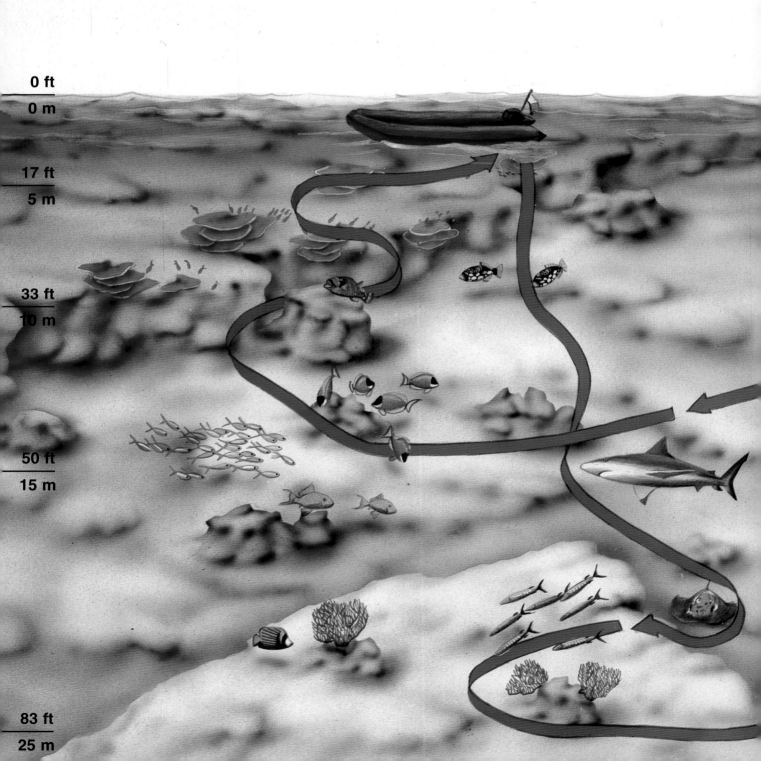

0 ft
0 m

17 ft
5 m

33 ft
10 m

50 ft
15 m

83 ft
25 m

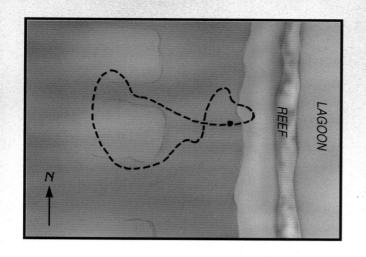

LAGOON

REEF

N

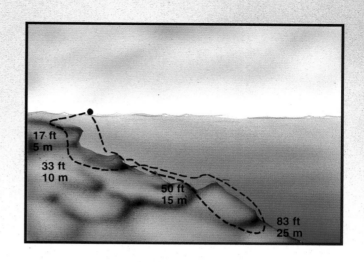

17 ft
5 m

33 ft
10 m

50 ft
15 m

83 ft
25 m

A

B

D

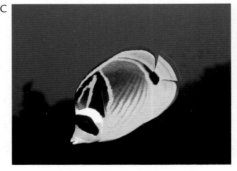

C

A. A stingray lies half-buried in the sandy seabed about 60 feet (18 meters) below the surface at Fa'a Miti.

B, C. Along the reef at Fa'a Miti and especially at the summit, one will find a large number of splendidly colored tropical fish, such as the angelfish (top) and the butterflyfish (bottom).

D. The wealth of the waters at Fa'a Miti is highlighted in this picture: butterflyfish and yellow sea perches swim calmly under the coral formation.

E. Reefs exposed to the winds are often frequented by dense schools of pelagic fish. To get a glimpse of these creatures, divers should from time to time look away from the reef wall toward the open sea.

The northwestern part of the island of Huahine has no lagoon, and the coral barrier follows the shoreline at just a few feet into the water, creating what is called a fringe reef.

The area between the Avamoa Pass and the runway of the airport is generally protected from the swell and strong winds. The water here is very clear, and the underwater landscape features a gentle slope interrupted by large blocks of coral that make for a very pleasant dive. Fa'a Miti is a site that lends itself both to introductory and to advanced diving, when the current does not allow diving in the pass.

On the reef, the small drop-off marks the beginning of the outer slope. Divers descend into 35 to 40 feet (10 to 12 meters) of water over a semi-sandy, gently sloping bed, interrupted by large clusters of coral. The area is very well lit, and marine life is concentrated in small caves and dim recesses. As soon as they come into the water, however, divers are greeted by trigger-fish and yellow sea perches.

A little lower, at about 60 feet (18 meters), a large mound rises clearly from the bed. Divers must then turn right to follow a sandy canal that continues for a few yards. Divers often come across a large stingray half-buried in the sand. As the divers approach, it leaves the bed in a cloud of sand, to fall back several yards away. Parrotfish, surgeonfish, and groupers are always present, and each crevice holds some marine life.

Fa'a Miti is a diving site where anything can happen. Two or three small sharks frequently come to take a look at the divers, and it is not uncommon

E

to see more solitary species such as a large barracuda or a dogtooth tuna.

At a depth of about 82 feet (25 meters), you reach a large area full of mushroom-shaped porites coral, to the right. If you stop here for a minute, you might come across a few emperor fish, a magnificent emperor angelfish, or, if you are really lucky, even a sea turtle.

The entire dive can easily be undertaken in about forty minutes, allowing for a long decompression stop at a depth of between 10 and 17 feet (3 and 5 meters) along the reef.

From September to November, the migration season of the humpback whales, one can frequently hear their shrill calls during the dive.

AVAPEHI PASS

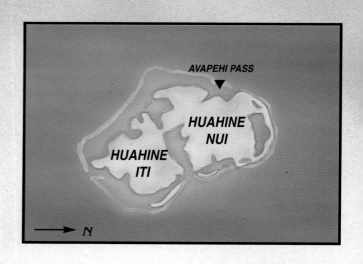

AVAPEHI PASS

HUAHINE NUI

HUAHINE ITI

N

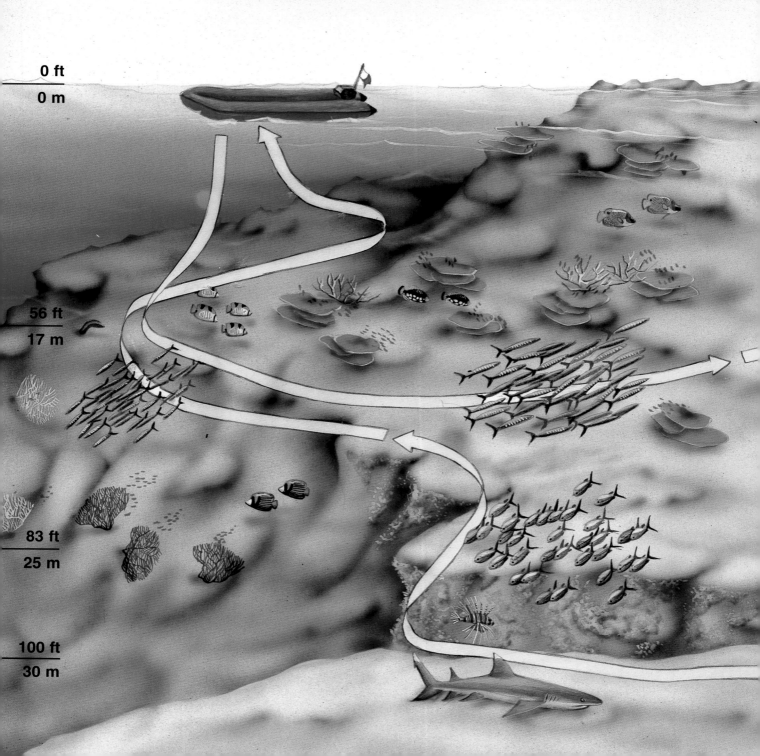

0 ft
0 m

56 ft
17 m

83 ft
25 m

100 ft
30 m

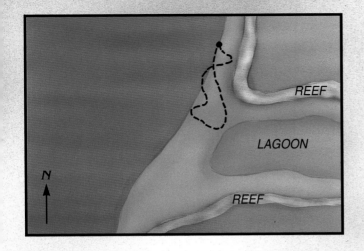

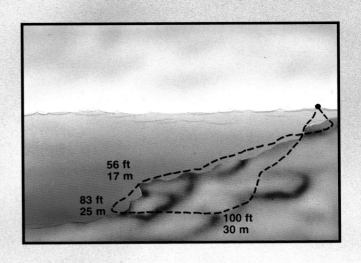

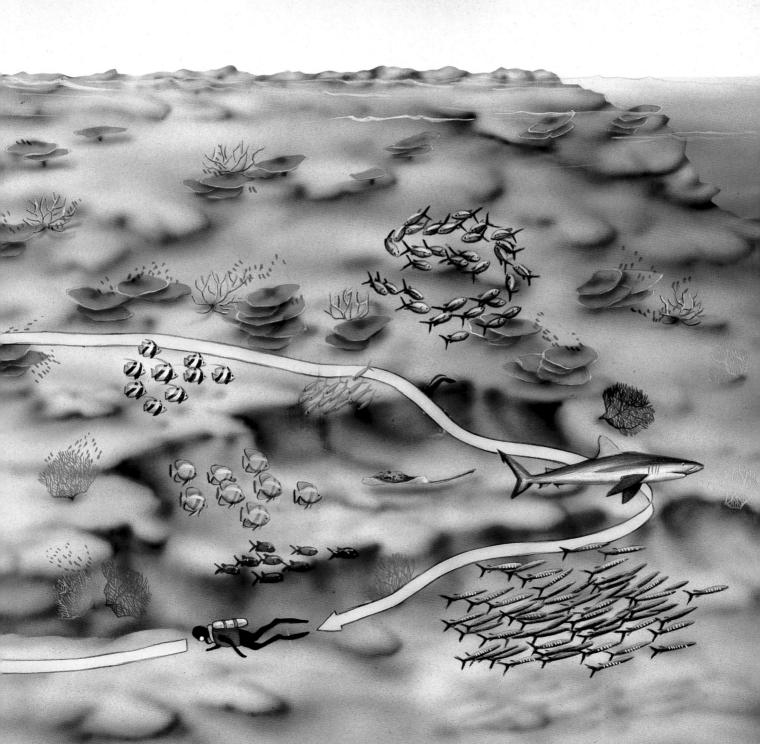

The Avapehi (or Fiti) Pass is situated off the west coast of Huahine, facing the villages of Fare and Fiti. About 330 yards (300 meters) wide and 130 feet (40 meters) deep, the pass is an excellent dive site, protected from the strong winds that blow here all year round. The alternating incoming and outgoing currents at the entrance to the lagoon are not generally strong. However, in certain weather conditions, the outgoing tide can sometimes be quite strong, forcing the divemaster to change the route of the diving excursion.

Marine life is densest with an outgoing current. However, as with most passes, the incoming current provides for excellent visibility, and although underwater life is less dense, one can admire the magnificent coral and splendid sunlit landscape.

The site is just three minutes by dinghy from the coast. A buoy marks the point of immersion. The dive starts by following the coral wall toward the pass, at a depth of about 50 feet (15 meters).

From the outset, a few regularly fed fish such as triggerfish or surgeonfish accompany the divers, and one or two gray sharks may make their appearance to satisfy their innate curiosity. Divers can come up close to a docile

this area. As a solitary tuna passes by, schools of perches disappear toward the lagoon.

The sandy bottom at the mouth of the pass, at a depth of about 100 feet (30 meters), slopes gently toward the open sea. A wall covered by very beautiful yellow stylaster coral can be seen on the right.

Following the wall at a depth of 83 feet (25 meters), one comes across a large number of holes that are home to mullets and angelfish. A few fin kicks upward, and the divers reach the reef slope that leads to the dive boat.

A. A grouper lies motionless, waiting to ambush unsuspecting prey.

B. Avapehi Pass, located on the west side of Huahine, is about 330 yards (300 meters) long, and reaches a depth of 132 feet (40 meters). These waters are home to extraordinary marine creatures that are easily spotted, especially with an outgoing tide.

C. A small strangely colored moray eel peeks out of its den in the coral wall.

D. A school of silver-hued jacks, so dense that they practically block out sunlight, swims in front of the camera lens. The black fish in the background are surgeonfish, easily recognizable by their oval bodies.

E. It is not uncommon to come across a school of about twenty gray sharks swimming calmly, together with striped snapper, along the reef of the Avapehi Pass.

D

E

giant moray eel at a depth of about 55 feet (17 meters).

At the corner of the pass, the vertical coral wall becomes a slight slope that ends in a plateau at the center of the pass to gently slope toward the open sea. These shallows disturb the current, creating slight turbulence that attracts a large number of species. This is why, with an outgoing current, in a few minutes one can come across splendid schools of mackerels, surgeonfish, and barracudas. Further below, it is not uncommon to sight a few batfish, and by looking upward one may come across a flight of honeycomb stingrays. Fifteen to twenty gray sharks frequent

The Island of Raiatea

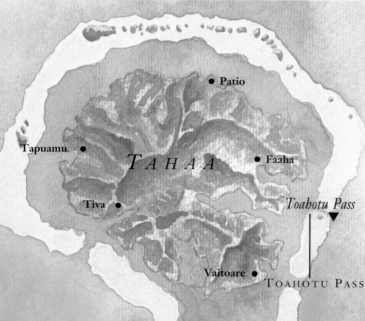

The second largest island of French Polynesia, lying 136 miles (220 kilometers) northwest of Tahiti, Raiatea has traditionally been considered the holy island from which the people of eastern Polynesia originated.

Here, high mountains seem to be the most important landmarks: Mount Temehani rises to 2,547 feet (772 meters). There are no sand beaches. Sunbathers in the lagoon use the many small reef islets, known as motus, scattered in front of the island.

Raiatea shares its lagoon and coral reef with the island of Tahaa. This island is more or less round, with a diameter of about 9 miles (15

C. The coral belt that surrounds the Raiatea lagoon—in the background here—is interrupted by a large number of passes.

D. The Toahotu Pass on the coral belt surrounding the smaller island of Tahaa.

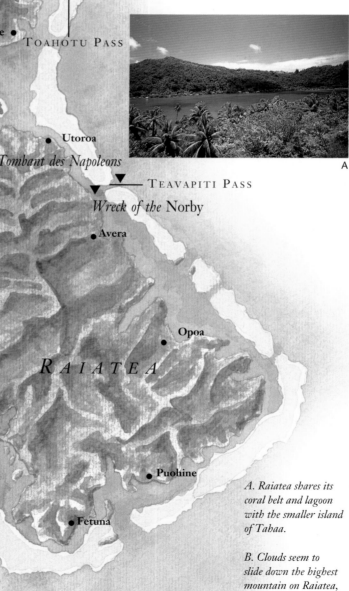

A. Raiatea shares its coral belt and lagoon with the smaller island of Tahaa.

B. Clouds seem to slide down the highest mountain on Raiatea, Mount Temehani, 2,547 feet (772 meters) above sea level.

A

B

kilometers), while Raiatea is 14 miles (22 kilometers) long and about 6 miles (10 kilometers) wide. According to local legend, the two were once a single island, divided by a giant eel. The Leeward Island does not only attract divers; with its excellent winds, it is also a paradise for sailing and surfing enthusiasts.

HISTORY

Raiatea was the cultural and religious as well as political center of Eastern Polynesia. It is believed that the long sea voyages of the Polynesians, who went as far as Hawaii and New Zealand,

started from here. Amongst European explorers, Captain James Cook seems to have had a special fondness for the island, since he visited it three times. Up until 1897, the people of Raiatea vehemently resisted French efforts of annexation.

DIVING

The coral belt around the lagoon at Raiatea is cut by several passes that make for excellent diving. Furthermore, the wreck of the *Norby*, one of the few wrecks accessible to divers in French Polynesia, is easily reached from the island.

TOAHOTU PASS

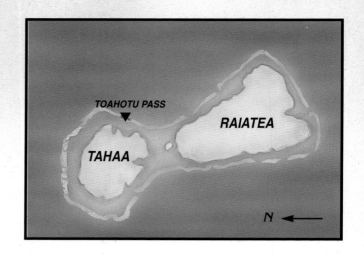

TOAHOTU PASS

TAHAA

RAIATEA

N

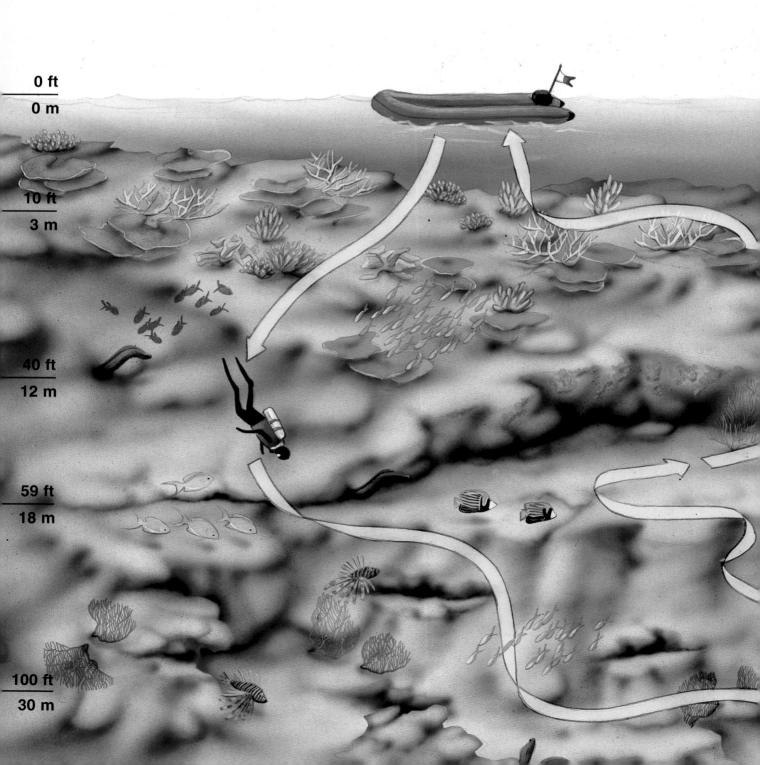

0 ft
0 m

10 ft
3 m

40 ft
12 m

59 ft
18 m

100 ft
30 m

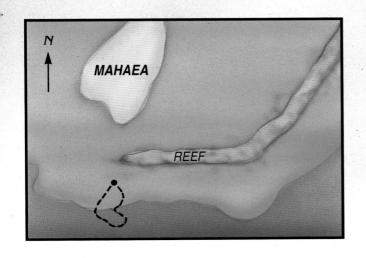

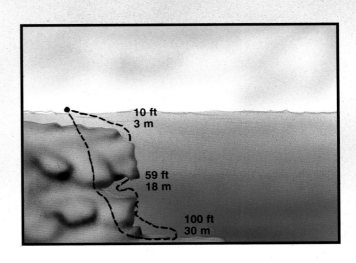

10 ft
3 m

59 ft
18 m

100 ft
30 m

A

B

C

A. At the bottom of the pass, a rare lemon shark is sometimes accompanied by one or two blacktip sharks.

B. Because of strong currents, Toahotu Pass is only suitable for experienced divers.

C. With an outgoing tide, one often encounters dense schools of pelagic fish, such as these mackerels, which swim together with a few surgeonfish.

D. The reef shelters a wide variety of marine creatures, such as this moray eel, which is really worthwhile seeing up close.

E. Toahotu Pass is often visited by large, solitary barracudas.

F. A dense shoal of bluestriped snappers at the bottom of the pass.

G. Aerial view showing the motus facing Toahotu Pass.

The Toahotu Pass, also known as Ceran, is in fact situated facing the bay of Haamene on the island of Tahaa. One of the most beautiful passes of this huge lagoon, the natural canal is known for its violent and sudden currents, and no diving party should venture out without a trained dive guide. Diving with an outgoing current is to be avoided at all costs.

Diving is done vertically from the point of anchorage, about 50 feet (15 meters) before the green buoy. Many species of colorful reef fish meet

D

E

the divers as soon as they go underwater, to gradually descend along the wall of the pass, which is full of holes encrusted with yellow coral.

A variety of underwater creatures use these holes as refuge. One encounters many mullets, soldierfish, surgeonfish, mackerel, groupers, and moray eels. It is not uncommon to come across one or two splendid specimens of the rare emperor angelfish.

An impressive cave lies at a depth of between 40 and 60 feet (12 and 18 meters), but it is better to visit it on the way back to the surface. A little lower, a platform at 100 feet (30 meters) makes an excellent observatory, overlooking the entire pass. A few minutes here,

F

spent quietly waiting, facing the current, generally allows you to observe the passage of a few large pelagic fish, such as a dogtooth tuna or a huge solitary barracuda.

More frequently, the presence of divers attracts a very beautiful school of bigeye trevally and a school of surgeonfish. You also may find barracudas in tight formations and more rarely, with luck, a few batfish, a turtle, or a manta ray. The Toahotu Pass is not generally frequented by sharks during the day, but you can see one or two whitetip sharks in the holes, and more rarely a lemon shark at the bottom of the canal.

Resurfacing is a nonchalant affair,

G

with visits to the holes, one after the other, as well as a little time in the cave at a depth of 40 to 60 feet (12 to 18 meters). The opening of the cave is rather high, but it narrows sharply toward the end. It is worthwhile to use a flashlight while visiting the cave to admire the yellow corals that line the ceiling and the walls. These corals, which are very sought after by collectors, are protected by special laws. The cave is home to a large number of fish species such as surgeonfish, angelfish, and groupers. The cave also features black arborescent coral.

The diving excursion ends calmly on the plateau at 10 to 13 feet (3 to 4 meters from the surface.

TOMBANT DES NAPOLEONS

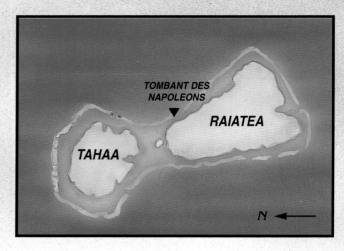

TOMBANT DES NAPOLEONS

TAHAA

RAIATEA

N

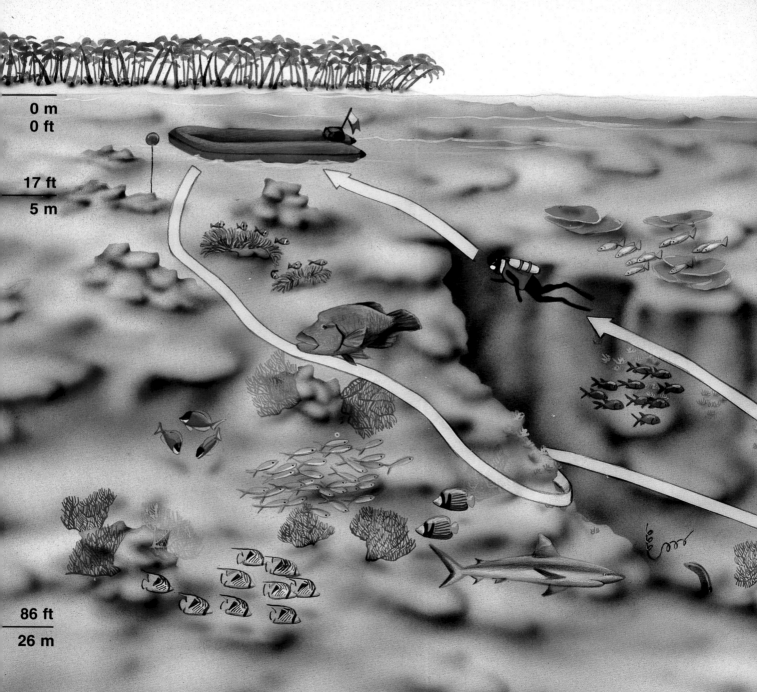

0 m
0 ft

17 ft
5 m

86 ft
26 m

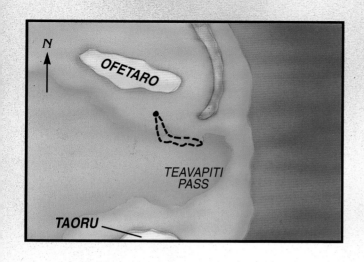

OFETARO

N

TEAVAPITI
PASS

TAORU

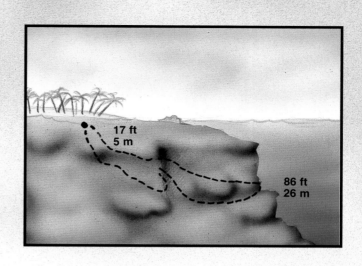

17 ft
5 m

86 ft
26 m

A

R aiatea and Tahaa are two high islands that are peculiar in that they are both situated in the same lagoon on a north-south axis. Eleven passes connect the lagoon with the ocean, playing an important role in the balance of the ecosystem as they allow the water of the lagoon to be refreshed. The walls of these passes are encrusted in certain areas with yellow, blue, or white coral.

The Tombant des Napoléons ("drop-off of the Napoleon wrasse") lies on the right flank of the Teavapiti Pass on the eastern coast of Raiatea. The peculiarity of this pass is that it is divided in two by the small islet Toaru

B

(*teavapiti* in Tahitian means "the two passes").

The dive site, just a three-minute boat ride off the coast, is marked by a surface buoy. Diving can be undertaken with an outgoing current, provided that it is not too strong, but ideal conditions are found after one or two

C

hours of incoming current.

After you enter the water, toward the center of the pass, you will see that a few coral formations have broken off from the reef. The drop-off or tombant lies about 65 feet (20 meters) farther, toward the mouth. A school of snappers (*Lutjanus monostignus*) and trumpet

the reef in parallel rows.

At a depth of 85 feet (26 meters), a peak juts out of the wall. Its width and inclination allow divers to stop on it for a while to observe the underwater landscape, since it affords an excellent view of the mouth of the pass. When the water is very clear, the sandy seabed at the foot of the wall reflects the light coming from the surface. The underwater scenery is spectacular, a joy for any photographer. Divers here often come across a solitary tuna or large barracuda, a school of mackerel, or, more often, a good half-dozen gray sharks, which may be fed, with caution.

At this point the current accelerates slightly, and the dive guide should start turning back, to follow the wall at a depth of between 50 to 65 feet (15 to 20 meters).

It is amusing to observe the few branches of stringy black coral, which look like giant springs in the water. Once again Napoleon wrasse follow the divers, and perches, surgeonfish, and trumpet emperors accompany the divers until they resurface.

Once back to the reef, the dive ends in 10 to 13 feet (3 or 4 meters) of water, where divers can use up their remaining air observing clownfish at home in their anemones.

F

G

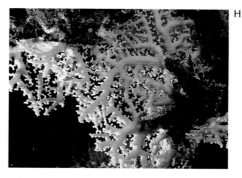

H

emperors (*Lethrinus miniatus*) generally accompanies the divers to this point, under the inquisitive eye of three or four Napoleon wrasse and blacktip sharks. The divers then go gradually deeper, following the wall. The area teems with large-eyed mullets and soldierfish. Every nook and cranny holds some sea life: giant moray eels, triggerfish, emperor angelfish, and groups of three to four butterflyfish. After a depth of about 65 feet (20 meters), the density of yellow and blue coral is remarkable. Their branches are not much bigger than a hand, but it is interesting to note their arrangement, aligned with

D

E

A. Teavapiti Pass, on the eastern coast of Raiatea. The Tombant des Napoléons lies to the right of the pass.

B. This site is famous for its Napoleon wrasse, which are not afraid of divers and often follow diving parties.

C. On the bottom of the pass one often finds a large solitary jacks.

D, E. Teavapiti Pass is home to extraordinary marine creatures such as the colorful royal angelfish (D) or a shy clownfish (E).

F. A shoal of snappers, accompanied by a few butterflyfish, swims around the pass in search of food.

G. Gray sharks are among the most typical inhabitants of the pass.

H. The walls of the pass are covered by a dense growth of multicolored coral.

THE WRECK OF THE NORBY

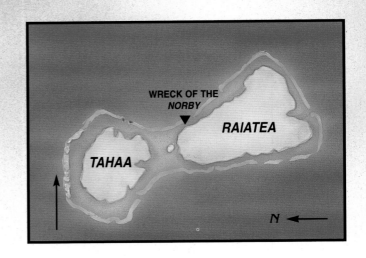

WRECK OF THE
NORBY

RAIATEA

TAHAA

N

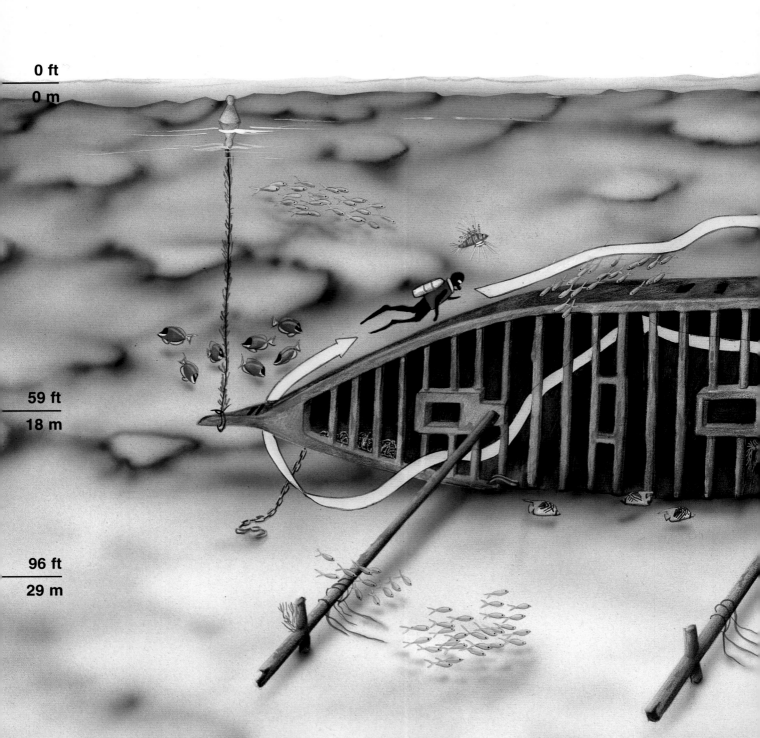

0 ft
0 m

59 ft
18 m

96 ft
29 m

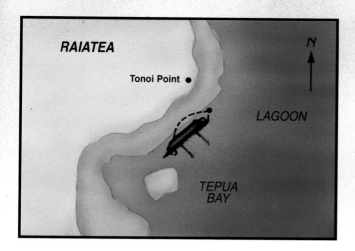

RAIATEA

Tonoi Point

N

LAGOON

TEPUA BAY

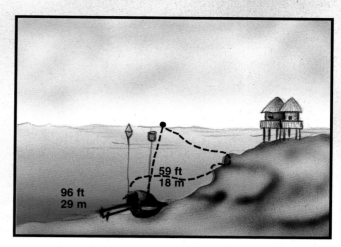

59 ft
18 m

96 ft
29 m

A

B

C

Because of its peculiar underwater topography, French Polynesia has very few wrecks accessible to divers. The wreck of the *Norby* lies in the Tepua Bay, facing the Teavapiti Pass, on the eastern coast of Raiatea.

The former three-mast vessel, which dates to the end of the nineteenth century, lies in the sludge on its port side at a depth of about 82 feet (25 meters). Very easy to locate, it lies close to the bungalows on stilts that make up the Hawaiki-Nui Hotel. Two surface buoys anchored to the ends of the vessel, which is 165 feet (50 meters) long and 50 feet (15 meters) wide, mark its precise location. Its wooden bridge and mizzenmast have completely disappeared, but all its metal structures are intact, making the *Norby* the best-preserved wreck in Polynesia.

The lagoon is always very calm at the site except after southeastern wind. The famous "Maraamu" blows in July and August, causing a strong surface chop and reducing visibility. Some-times, however, the wind blows from the west for several days, creating ideal conditions and rendering the *Norby* visible even from the surface.

A visit to the wreck starts from the rear of the ship. After going around the rudder blade, divers can enter the hull between two metal beams. Many

cloud of mullets occupy the inner part of the bow, just before the exit, where at the limit of the vessel, large auriga butterflyfish swim in pairs.

As you leave the vessel at about 60 feet (18 meters), the two remaining masts come into view. Partially broken, they are still in their original location. After going around the bow, divers return to the rear of the hull.

Air supply permitting, it is very interesting to gradually ascend the mass of fallen rock that leads to the foot of the stilted bungalows and to resurface in 10 feet (3 meters) of water, in an area teeming with a large number of species of lagoon fish, nudibranchs, and small crustaceans.

While the atmosphere of a wreck dive is the main attraction of diving here during the day, night diving is best for observing all the underwater life on and around the *Norby*.

C. The reef close to the Norby *is home to colorful creatures such as this grouper, accompanied by a few perches.*

D. A diver peeks out of a porthole of the Norby.

E. Good light and the flash of a camera illuminate the colorful fish that inhabit the wreck. Here, a school of red perch swims around the main anchor chain.

F. The sheet anchor located inside the three-masted vessel that sank in the waters off Raiatea in August 1900.

A. A diver approaches the remains of the metal structure of the bridge of the Norby.

B. Divers can easily penetrate the wreck, passing between metal bars on the bridge. The Norby, *though completely bare, is interesting for the multicolored marine life that has colonized it. The picture shows a moorish idol.*

underwater species have their homes in the deepest areas of the wreck: mullets, perches, a large number of shrimps, and in particular, a few groupers. The entire wreck is covered with silt, and care must be taken while moving around it so as not to disturb deposited sediments that could greatly reduce underwater visibility. The upper part of the hull is padded with dendrophyllia coral in many colors, and it is amusing to watch the fish swim among the coral. The inside of the vessel is well lit, and so a flashlight is not a must. Divers can go in and out of the vessel at any time, since the blue of the sea is always visible.

The central part of the hull is not very rich in fish, although it is colonized by stringy black coral. It is not uncommon to come across one or two large jacks of the family Carangidae. Farther ahead, an air pocket bears witness to the regular visits of divers. It is even large enough to allow divers to remove their masks and exchange a few words underwater.

A little lower, toward the bow, the anchor—still clinging to the bottom—is covered with coral. The chain, which is still visible, is home to an enormous moray eel that seems to have become the eternal guardian of the wreck. A

The Island of Bora Bora

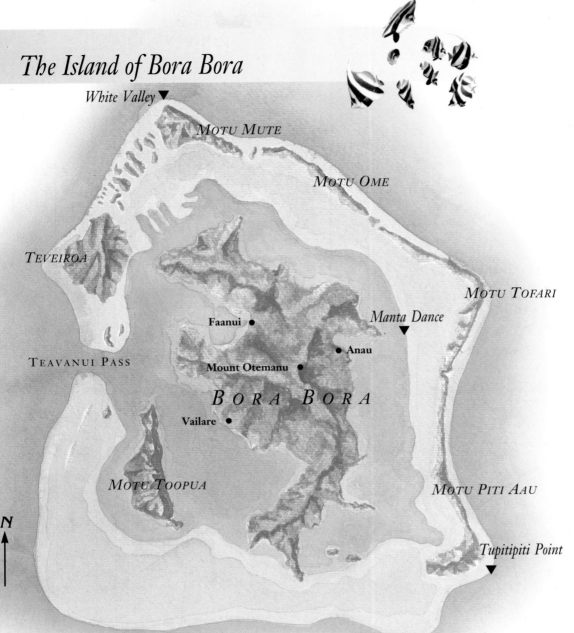

White Valley ▼

MOTU MUTE

MOTU OME

TEVEIROA

MOTU TOFARI

Faanui •

Manta Dance ▼

• Anau

Mount Otemanu •

TEAVANUI PASS

B O R A   B O R A

Vailare •

MOTU TOOPUA

MOTU PITI AAU

N

Tupitipiti Point ▼

C. In the background, the Otemanu volcano rises 2,399 feet (727 meters) above sea level to dominate the lush green island of Bora Bora.

D. The island's unrivaled landscape has made Bora Bora a popular tourist destination since the late 1960s.

B

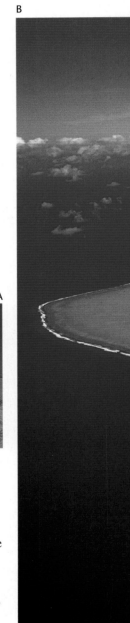

A. An outrigger canoe lies on the beach at Bora Bora, by far the most famous atoll in the Society Islands.

B. Aerial view of the main island of Bora Bora and the large number of motus, small pieces of coral belt rising above the surface and the extraordinary lagoon.

Bora Bora is the best known and most photographed island of French Polynesia. The 6-mile (10-kilometer)-long main island is surrounded by a splendid lagoon, in which there are a few motus, as small islets are called. Bora Bora is surrounded by a coral reef that has only one connection to the sea, allowing ships to pass. The island's emblem is surely the volcano Mount Otemanu, which from its height of 2,399 feet (727 meters) dominates the lush slopes of the island and the lagoon shimmering with a wide range of colors.

The large airport, built by the Americans during World War II, lies at Motu Mute, at the northernmost

A

end of the island. Not far from the runway one of the best dive sites of Bora Bora, White Valley, lies here. The largest settlement on the island is Vaitape, where incoming tourists arrive by boat from the airport. Bora Bora was the first tourist resort in French Polynesia, and today it is overrun with hotels, restaurants, and shops.

HISTORY

The first inhabitants of the islands were warriors who often attacked the neighboring islands of Tahaa and Raiatea. The island was discovered in 1722 by the Dutchman Roggeveen, who was followed fifty-five years later by James Cook. In 1895 the island was annexed by France. During World War II the Americans hurriedly set up a base here, referred to by the code name "Bobcat." The airport also dates to this period. The fact that many of the older islanders speak good "American" can be attributed to their contact with the over 4,000 U.S. troops still stationed on the island.

DIVING

Diving at Bora Bora can be undertaken both in the lagoon and on the outer side of the reef, offering the advantage of allowing diving in all weather and sea conditions. The lagoon is extremely rich in fish and is the natural habitat of countless manta rays, which attract visitors to the Calypso Club diving center with their "Manta dance." Introductory diving is possible in the lagoon, although more experience is required for the outer side of the reef.

Diving in Bora Bora is regulated by international and French Polynesian standards.

C

D

WHITE VALLEY

BORA BORA

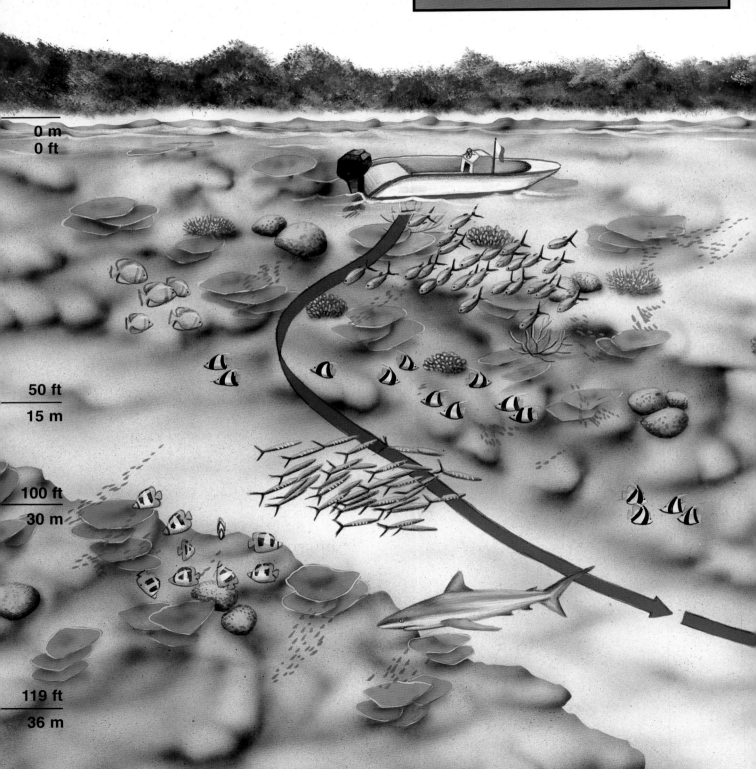

0 m
0 ft

50 ft
15 m

100 ft
30 m

119 ft
36 m

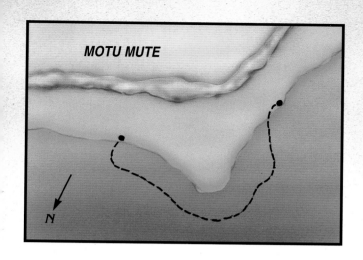

MOTU MUTE

N

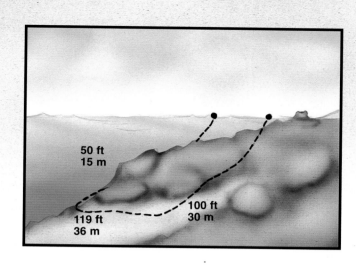

50 ft
15 m

119 ft
36 m

100 ft
30 m

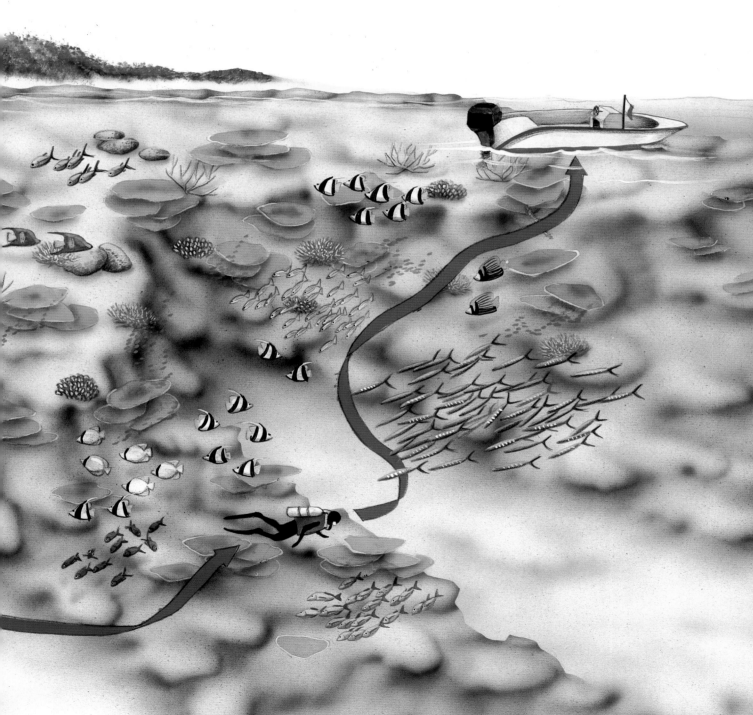

A

The diving site White Valley is located in front of the Bora Bora airport, built by the Americans during World War II, on Motu Mute. Access to the site is by boat, heading north after the pass along the northwestern part of the reef. As with all outer reefs, diving is dependent on the wind. South and east winds ensure that the water around White Valley is calm and crystal clear. To get a better view of the area, visitors should go in for a long boat ride following the current. After entering the water, the boat anchored above the coral platform that lies about 35 feet (10 meters) below the surface, divers should descend along the reef slope to reach the sandy

A. A group of divers heading by boat toward White Valley, a dive site on the outer reef, off the northern coast of Bora Bora.

B. The waters of White Valley are home to a large number of Polynesian reef-dwelling species, such

as these bluestriped snappers, with their distinctive yellow-and-blue pattern.

C. At the coral wall at White Valley, a diver tries to capture a few surgeonfish on film.

B

bottom at a depth of about 100 feet (30 meters). This strip of white sand runs parallel to the reef and then slopes toward the deep where the part of the reef facing the open sea forms a projection. Divers should swim around this underwater promontory to reach another sandy strip running parallel to the coral wall. The dive consists in following the sandy path. Depending on remaining air reserves and bottom time, the divers may choose to resurface on the reef platform. This dive should only be attempted by advanced divers, since the depth and the exposed position of the reef requires greater skill than the calm waters inside the lagoon. The reef is inhabited by all the

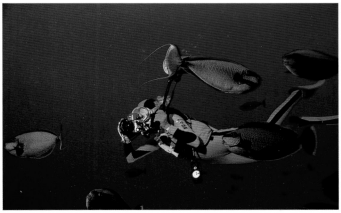

C

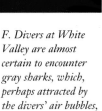

D. The turquoise water is an excellent backdrop to the yellow snappers in the foreground.

E. Large solitary jacks are not uncommon on the outer reef.

F. Divers at White Valley are almost certain to encounter gray sharks, which, perhaps attracted by the divers' air bubbles, come up from the deep for brief appearances.

D

F

E

usual creatures found on Polynesian reefs: surgeonfish, Napoleon wrasse, triggerfish, and shoals of snappers. Close to the sandy bottom, divers will come across a large number of garden eels *(Heteroconger hassi)*, which seem to stand like giant asparagus in the sand. However, it is impossible to approach them since they are shy and disappear into the sand as soon as the surrounding water is disturbed. Stingrays can be seen half-buried in the sand, and when the current is strong, blacktip sharks bask motionless in the flow of water just outside the reef. At Tiputa Pass in the Rangiroa atoll, one can see

hundreds of almost motionless sharks caressed by the strong current that forces oxygen-rich water through their gills. Smaller sharks such as the whitetip seem to be able to obtain sufficient oxygen even when they are immobile and close to the bottom, and other shark species have highly developed gill muscles that allow them to breathe without swimming. Apart from whitetip sharks, divers at White Valley will also encounter gray reef sharks that, attracted from the deep by the noise of the divers' air bubbles, venture briefly into shallower waters.

When diving at White Valley, one should also keep an eye on the open sea, where it is not uncommon to spot large schools of jacks, tuna, and silver-hued barracuda. As in all areas exposed to a constant current, White Valley features a rich and varied growth of coral. Divers shouldn't miss the opportunity to admire this extraordinary life form.

MANTA DANCE

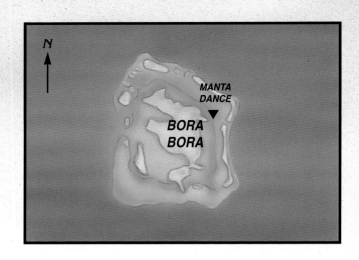

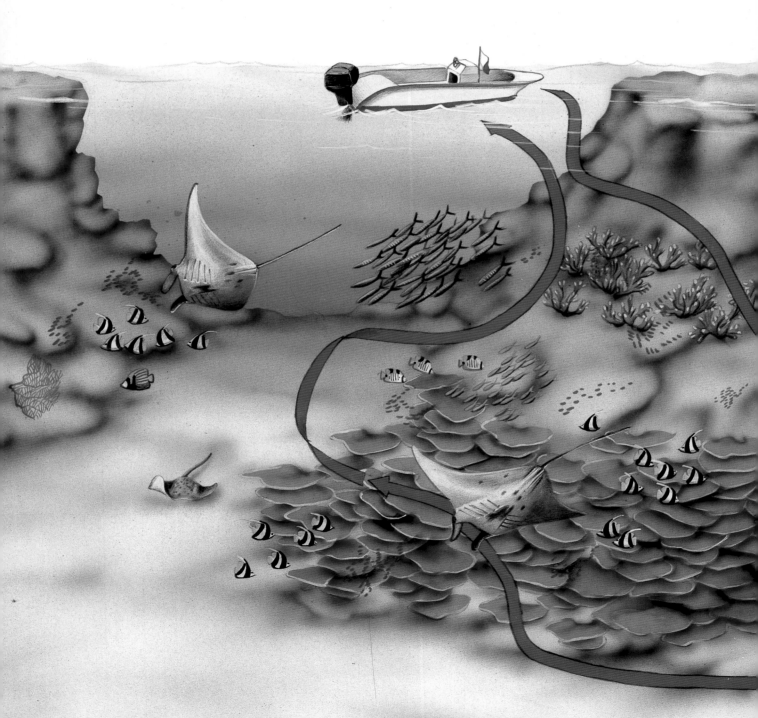

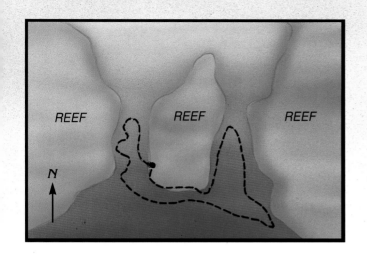

REEF REEF REEF

N

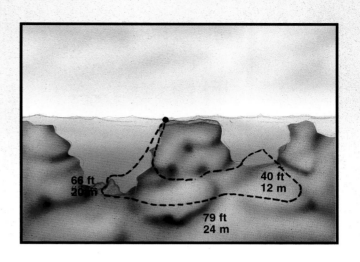

66 ft
20 m

40 ft
12 m

79 ft
24 m

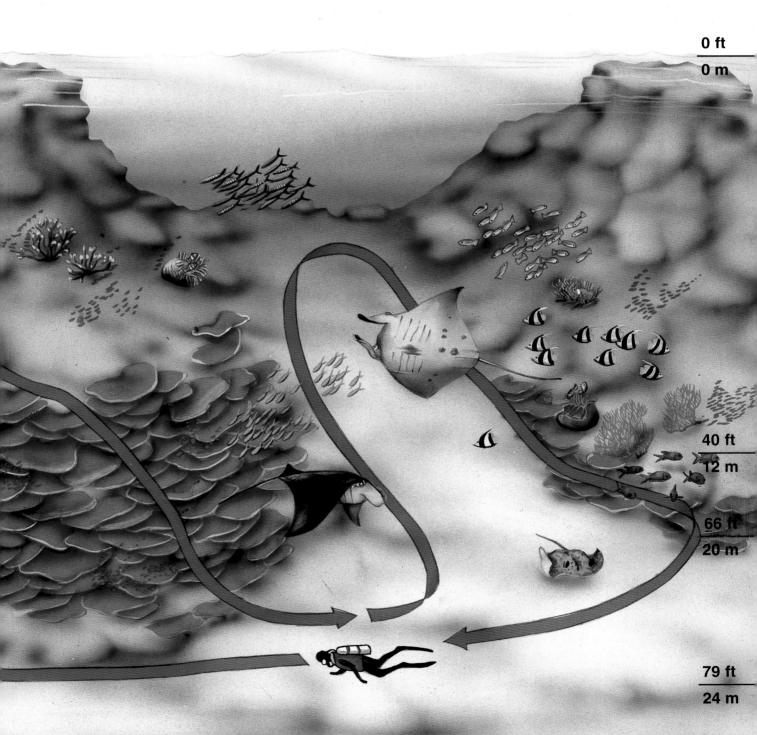

0 ft

0 m

40 ft

12 m

66 ft

20 m

79 ft

24 m

The Manta Dance dive site is located inside the lagoon at Bora Bora. The manta rays from which the site takes its name owe their presence to the light and constant current, which brings in plankton-rich water.

Leaving the jetty of the Calypso Club to proceed northward, one can see the reef just under the water, marked by two buoys. Divers should enter the water near the huge coral structure, which lies at a 45-degree angle in the middle of two passes. The sandy bottom slopes downward to the south up to 80 feet (24 meters). This site can be dived by one and all, regardless of experience. The coral formation slopes downward at an angle that allows divers to stop their descent at the desired diving depth. Furthermore, unlike at the outer reef, behind

A. A diver carrying food is nearly overcome by a group of various fish.

B. Even isolated coral formations are home to interesting life forms, such as this huge moray eel.

C. Bora Bora is a natural paradise both above and below the water.

D. Close to the sandy bottom, the reef at Manta Dance is covered by an expanse of montipore coral.

E. Manta Dance owes its name to the manta rays that are common in these waters.

F. Manta Dance lies inside the Bora Bora lagoon, where one often finds large pelagic fish, such as this barracuda.

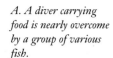

C

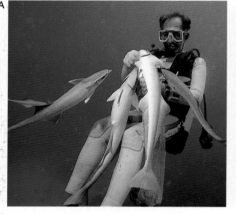

A

D

B

the inner reef the current is not very strong, and waves do not pose a problem.

The boat is generally anchored at the fixed buoys located close to the reef. From this point, divers should follow the sloping reef up to the sandy bottom at 80 feet (24 meters) below the surface. If the dive plan allows, and encounters with manta rays and other marine creatures do not distract the divers too much, they can swim around the coral formation with the dive guide. At the foot of this coral formation, facing south, is an expanse totally overgrown by very fragile montipore coral. Divers should take care not to damage these delicate creatures, by not touching the coral-covered reef.

The main attraction at Manta Point is obviously the manta rays. These enormous fish, also known as devilfish, seem to exert a particular charm over divers. The nickname follows a legend that when seamen first saw these extraordinary creatures, they thought they were devils from the deep which seemed to want to capture the anchor chain with their horns while flapping their fins, giving the impression that they were trying to capsize the vessel. When the "devil" abandoned the anchor chain close to the surface, it turned, showing off its huge mouth and white belly in clear contrast to its dark back. This inexplicable behavior was repeated

several times, to the horror of super-stitious sailors who believed that these creatures were trying to drag the entire ship and its crew toward some underwater hell.

Manta rays are in fact harmless creatures, although they can grow to a considerable size, sometimes attaining wingspans of 13 feet (4 meters). The strange movement of their horns—that is, their cephalic fins—against the chains of ships' anchors is easily explained: These fish use chains and ropes to rid themselves of parasites, especially on their cephalic fins, which are partic-ularly sensitive. At Manta Point, divers can watch these sea giants at leisure as they flit about elegantly in the water.

However, Manta Point also holds other delights in store. The site is an underwater paradise populated by a large number of lively-hued tropical species, and a school of remoras often accompanies divers. Stingrays can be seen half-buried in the sand, while whitetip sharks cruise nervously close to the reef, and smaller gray sharks swim nearby.

Manta Point is also famous for its constant large population of moray eels and barracudas. The latter are inquisitive by nature; when sunlight reflecting off diving equipment gives away the presence of divers, they follow the party throughout the dive. Unfortunately, giant barracudas are no

longer to be found, although together with manta rays they once abounded in these waters. Lastly, in the two sandy passes one can easily find honeycomb stingrays and sea anemones that have colonized coral formations.

F

TUPITIPITI POINT

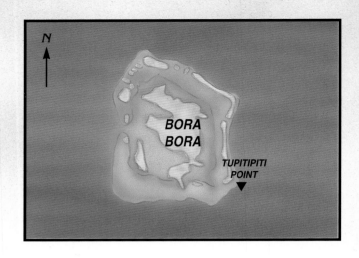

BORA
BORA

TUPITIPITI
POINT

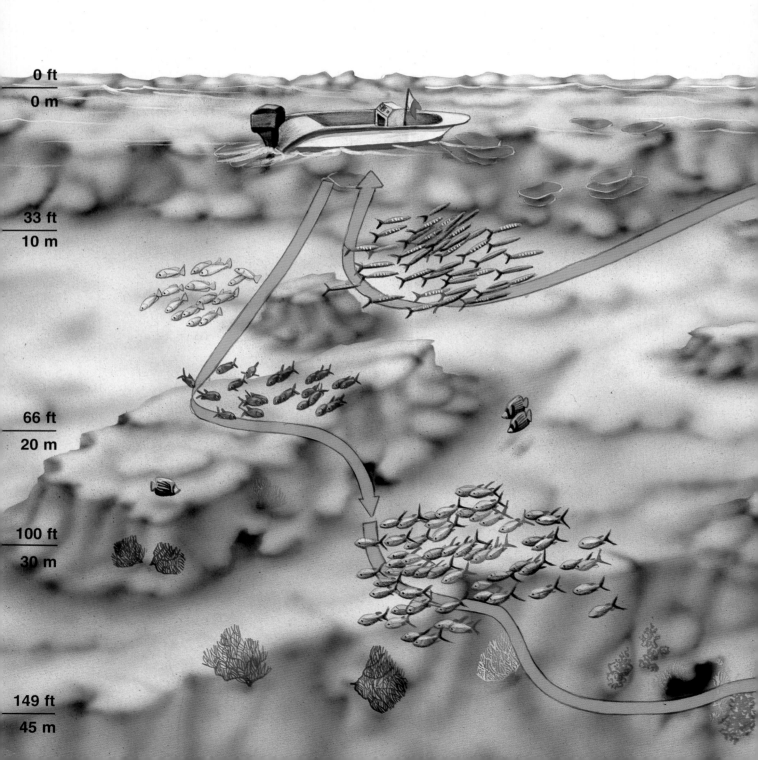

0 ft
0 m

33 ft
10 m

66 ft
20 m

100 ft
30 m

149 ft
45 m

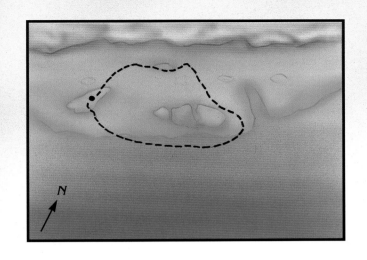

N

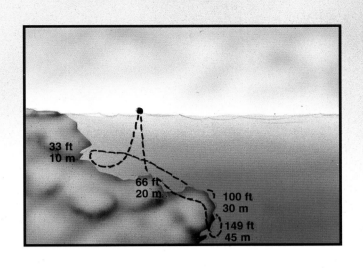

33 ft
10 m

66 ft
20 m

100 ft
30 m

149 ft
45 m

Tupitipiti Point lies on the outer reef off the southeastern tip of Bora Bora. Since the only pass linking the lagoon to the open sea lies at the center of the eastern side of the atoll, the boat ride to Tupitipiti Point is quite long. Weather and wind conditions affect both diving and the duration of the boat trip. With an east wind, diving is impossible; with a south wind, the dive site a little more turbulent than with a north or a west wind. The reef, which almost touches the surface of the water, forms a vertical wall that drops off for 33 feet (10 meters) to meet a platform featuring large coral formations. At the end of this plateau, the reef falls

of marine creatures. To fully enjoy these delights, all divers in these waters should carry a flashlight. The dive at Tupitipiti Point could end by following the coral wall up to a depth of between 30 to 10 feet (9 to 3 meters).

Tupitipiti Point is extraordinarily rich in biodiversity. The walls are covered by tiny, mostly purple-hued coral branches. Large multicolored corals can be found even at depths of 145 feet (44 meters), as in the caves mentioned. Thanks to its position on the outer reef, thus exposed to strong currents, Tupitipiti Point is often frequented by large pelagic fish. Whitetip and blacktip sharks can be found close to the platform at 30 feet

off steeply toward the deep. Here the water is generally crystal clear, and the brightly sunlit underwater landscape contrasts with the blue deep.

In calm seas, the boat should be anchored to one of the large rock formations. Divers can also choose to do a drift dive in the current; in this case the surface vessel will follow the divers and pick them up at the end of the dive. The diving limit is 145 feet (44 meters); at this depth are underwater caves, whose walls are carpeted with multicolored corals. Given the great depth, however, only experienced divers should attempt a visit to these caves. Tupitipiti Point nevertheless has plenty in store even for beginners, who can swim along the coral wall at a depth of 80 feet (24 meters), or among the coral formations on the platform.

The crevices in the reef and vertical walls are livened by the bright colors of marine flora, home to a wide variety

A. The reef at Tupitipiti Point features huge coral formations, festooned by a large number of encrusting corals.

B. A diver examines a vertical wall covered in small sea fans at Tupitipiti Point.

C. The blue expanse of the deep is often illuminated by the silver flashes of certain schools of fish, such as these snappers.

(9 meters) or deeper. Looking toward the deep, divers will often see large schools of silvery jacks, which light up the dark with metallic flashes.

In the waters of Tupitipiti Point you may also find hammerhead sharks, rare in this part of French Polynesia. The ever-present barracudas are generally quite large and are to be found especially above the coral formations on the coral. Not in all seasons, but certainly in November and December, the area abounds in triggerfish. On the other hand, it is impossible to foresee with certainty when manta rays and eagle rays can be found here, since these creatures swim around the atoll, never remaining in a single location

for long, as they do in the passes.

Divers will focus on the underwater landscape and on the larger fish species, especially as bottom time is rather limited. On the platform and during the dive, you should nevertheless take a little time to observe the many tropical fish that keep close to the bottom, taking full advantage of the protection afforded by the of the reef, into which they disappear at the first sign of danger. Many of these fish have bright, lively colors and rather bizarre shapes.

The holes in the reef are home to a variety of crustaceans, especially lobsters, sea spiders, and various types of crabs. Being nocturnal creatures, crustaceans spend most of the day in their dens, coming out only after dark to scour the seabed.

D. The crevices of the reef shelter strangely colored and bizarrely shaped fish, such as this turkeyfish.

E. Close to the sandy bottom, where the reef drops off toward the deep, the coral formations are home to a large number of species that are well worth a close look. In the picture, a diver seems to be face to face with a moray eel.

F. A few young barracuda parade in front of the camera.

THE TUAMOTU ISLANDS

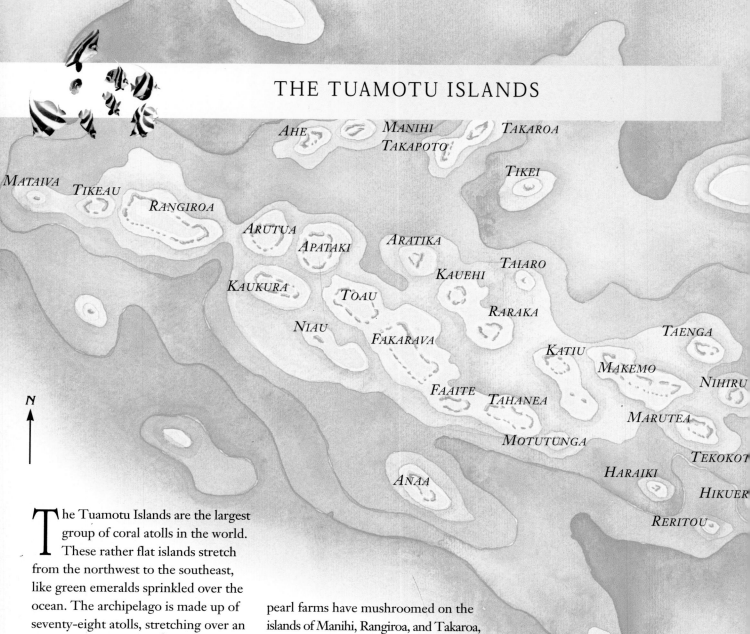

AHE   MANIHI   TAKAROA
TAKAPOTO

TIKEI

MATAIVA   TIKEAU

RANGIROA

ARUTUA

APATAKI   ARATIKA

KAUEHI   TAIARO

KAUKURA   TOAU   RARAKA

NIAU   FAKARAVA   TAENGA

KATIU   MAKEMO

FAAITE   NIHIRU

TAHANEA   MARUTEA

MOTUTUNGA   TEKOKOT

ANAA   HARAIKI   HIKUER

RERITOU

N

The Tuamotu Islands are the largest group of coral atolls in the world. These rather flat islands stretch from the northwest to the southeast, like green emeralds sprinkled over the ocean. The archipelago is made up of seventy-eight atolls, stretching over an area 744 miles (1,200 kilometers) long and 375 miles (600 kilometers) wide.

Most of the seventy-eight atolls have one or two canals through which the lagoons are supplied with water from the open sea. These cuts in the reef ring are also the best diving spots, since the nutrient-rich current attracts a large number of pelagic fish.

From time immemorial, the inhabitants of the Tuamotu Islands have lived off fishing and the processing of coconut palm products. However, pearl diving is also a major source of income. In the past, indigenous divers used to go to a depth of up to 100 feet (30 meters) to pick oysters without any equipment whatsoever. Today, the pearl are cultivated, and industrially organized

pearl farms have mushroomed on the islands of Manihi, Rangiroa, and Takaroa, among others. The black pearls of the Tuamotus are famous the world over.

HISTORY

The Tuamotu Islands were first settled in around 1000 A.D. The first settlers came from the Marquesas Islands and what are now called the Society Islands. The inhabitants of the islands were in constant conflict and even led military campaigns against the Society Islands. Even as Tahiti became a French protectorate in 1842, the Tuamotu Islands remained independent. The islands were first annexed when they became a French colony in 1880, together with the Society Islands. It is interesting to note that during the entire period of

A. In the waters of the Tuamotu Islands, especially along the reef outside the lagoon, it is common to encounter large marine predators.

B. Extraordinary underwater vegetation, made up of encrusting sponges and soft coral, covers the reef wall.

A

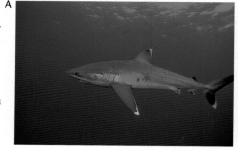

TEPOTO NAPUKA

C. Aerial view of some
of the many motus that
are a typical feature of
the Rangiroa Atoll.

D. The crystal waters
of the Rangiroa
Lagoon allow for
extraordinary
photographs.

C

D

PUKAPUKA

TAKUME

RAROIA

FANGATAU

FAKAINA

REKA REKA

TAUERE

AMANU

HAO

RAVAHERE

PUKARUA

REAO

AKIAKI

VAHITHAI

NENGO NENGO

MANUHANGI   PARAOA   NUKUTAVAKE

VAIRAATEA   PINAKI

AHUNUI

European colonization, no ship could throw anchor to make an occupational landing on the islands. All attempts were fiercely opposed by the islanders, who managed to protect their islands despite the fact that they were fighting with primitive weapons against forces using firearms.

It was in the Tuamotus, and precisely at the Raroia Atoll, that the *Kon Tiki* expedition led by the explorer Thor Heyerdahl—who wanted to prove that in remote times Peruvian Indians could have undertaken transoceanic sea voyages—came to an end. Heyerdahl's famous raft was dashed against a reef, after having traversed the 4,300 miles (7,000 kilometers) between South America and Polynesia in 101 days.

B

TUREIA

VANAVANA

The Island of Rangiroa

The Rangiroa atoll lies 125 miles (202 kilometers) northwest of Papeete. The second largest atoll in the world, its huge 620-square-mile (1,000-square-kilometer) emerald green lagoon stretches 48 miles (78 kilometers) long and 15 miles (24 kilometers) wide. *Rangiroa* means "open sky" in Polynesian, a fitting name, given that the other side of the atoll lies beyond sight.

The airstrip, on which the twin-engined aircraft of Air Tahiti land daily, lies 3 miles (5 kilometers) outside the little hamlet Avaturu. There is just one road that runs through the 12-mile (20-kilometer)-long island to link up with the Tiputa Pass. Nearly all the hotels in the area are located along this road, facing the lagoon.

The town of Tiputa lies on the other side of the Tiputa Pass. The two dive sites of the Raie Manta Club lie directly on the two canals to the Avaturu Pass and the Tiputa Pass. The trip takes only a few minutes on a powerful dinghy.

Diving is almost completely concentrated around these passes in the coral ring surrounding the island, both inside and outside the lagoon. Here divers are met with a very rich underwater fauna, from small tropical fish typical of reefs to large pelagic

A. Aerial view of the Avataru Pass, an unforgettable dive site.

B. The colors of the Polynesian islands are unique, from the bright green of the vegetation on the motus to the blinding white of the beaches and the extraordinary shades of blue of the lagoon and the open sea.

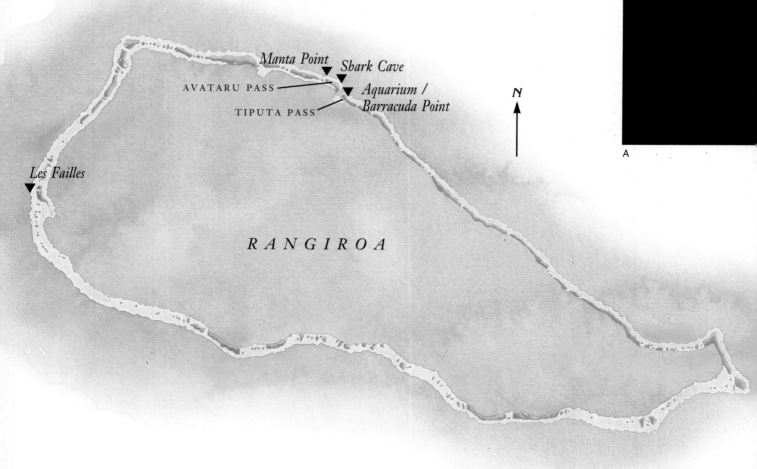

A

B

C

D

species, sea turtles, sharks, dense schools of fish, and dolphins.

Besides the passes, an area called Les Failles to the southwest of the outer reef at Rangiroa makes for excellent diving because of its spectacular topography.

Only drift diving is possible in the passes, and the dinghies follow the divers. All diving teams are equipped with self-inflating marker-buoys, which are sent to the surface at the end of the dive to signal the position of the divers.

As at almost all other dive sites in the region, safety rules are based on international and local French Polynesian standards.

C. The waters at Avataru Pass are often frequented by dense schools of pelagic species, especially jacks and small tuna.

D. Blacktip sharks are frequently found close to reef walls outside lagoons, finding easy prey in the fish-rich waters.

AQUARIUM

AQUARIUM

RANGIROA

LAGOON

N

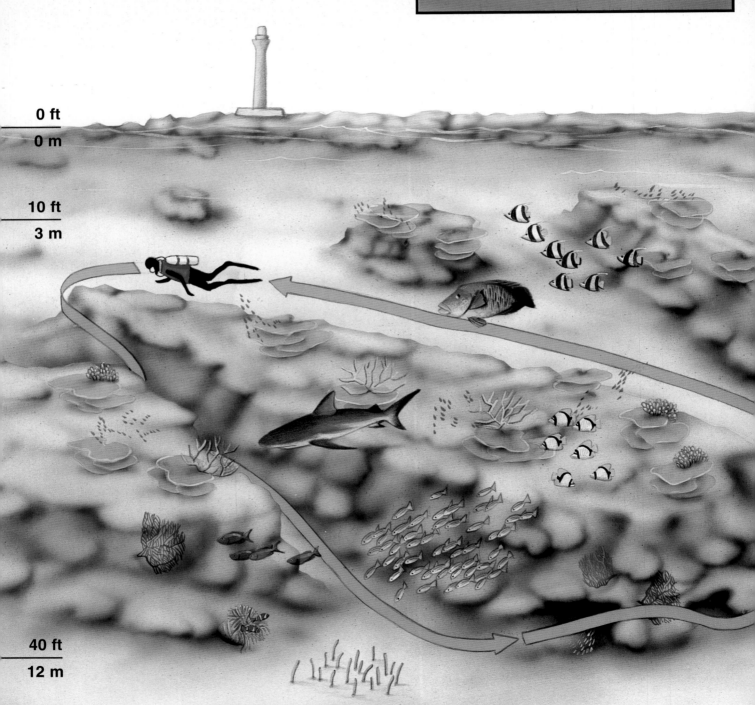

0 ft
0 m

10 ft
3 m

40 ft
12 m

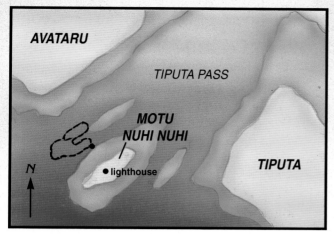

AVATARU

TIPUTA PASS

MOTU
NUHI NUHI

TIPUTA

N

lighthouse

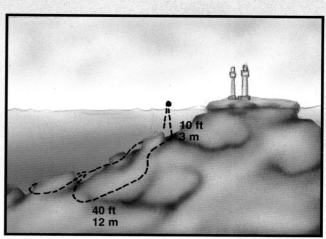

10 ft
3 m

40 ft
12 m

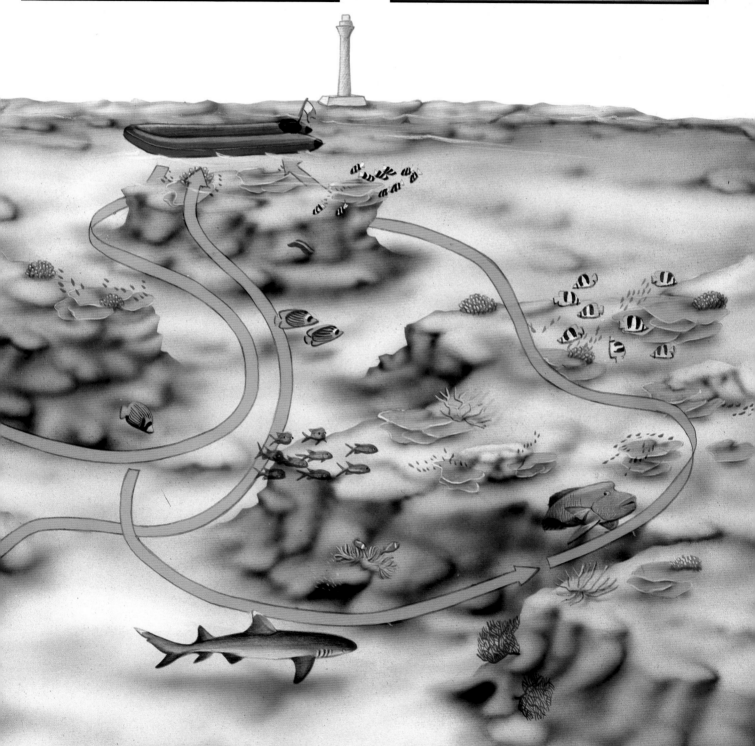

A

B

A. Aquarium is located inside the lagoon near Tiputa Pass, close to an isolated reef known as Motu Nuhi Nuhi. The picture shows various types of hard coral that cover the walls of the reef.

B. A diver, literally surrounded by a crowd of surgeonfish, tries to take a picture of a Napoleon wrasse.

C. Aquarium owes its name to the incredible variety of multicolored tropical fish species that populate its waters.

D. A moray eel peeks out of its den. Its open jaws are not meant to be intimidating; to breathe, moray eels must let oxygen-rich water flow through their open mouths.

E. At Aquarium, divers can admire the shy clownfish that are nearly always hidden among anemones' tentacles.

F. Only nature can be so generous: the green mantle of a tridacna contrasts with purple coral.

C

This dive site, known as Aquarium for its many multicolored tropical fish, lies at the end of the Tiputa Pass, inside the lagoon. A single unattached reef, known as Motu Nuhi Nuhi, rises toward the surface right in the middle of the Tiputa Pass, marked by two lighthouses.

The dive site, distinguishable by the large number of buoys to which boats are attached, lies to the west of the reef. Aquarium can be dived in all weather conditions, even when the incoming or outgoing tide reaches its peak, since the site is protected against the current by the coral reef. The reef extends westward in a flat plane toward the pass, and the surface is only slightly

roughened by the last huge coral rocks. The surface is also interrupted by ravines and crevices toward the part of the reef that emerges above the water. The maximum depth here is 40 feet (12 meters) even where the reef meets the sandy seabed, which extends without a further incline far into the lagoon.

Diving is also possible on the eastern side of Motu Nuhi Nuhi, although not at all times, since the reef is exposed to the current that is a typical feature of passes. The eastern wall of the reef is steep, and its coral overgrowth very beautiful.

Aquarium is an ideal dive site for beginners and first-timers. Underwater photographers also favor this area because they don't have to worry about bottom time, currents, and air reserves while photographing the most beautiful fish.

The site is aptly named. A huge school of black-and-white-striped sergeant majors awaits visitors just under the buoy. A group of snappers lives just above one of the coral formations that surround the sandy bed in which the buoy is anchored; as soon as the divers leave, the snappers swim in the boat's shadow on the seabed. Also just under the boat, moray eels stare out of the coral, but they are

harmless. Large numbers of varied, exotic coral fish can be seen without going very far. Already at the buoy, divers will come across butterflyfish, emperor fish, longfin bannerfish, surgeonfish, and triggerfish. Diving over the reef or through one of the crevices toward the west, you reach the edge where the coral rock drops steeply to meet the sandy seabed. The edge forms an over-hang in many areas and is the favorite spot of the nurse sharks and whitetip sharks that lie on the sandy seabed.

At the slope, swim southward, where the current is practically nil. Here you will be joined by Napoleon wrasse, who will follow the diving party.

Moving southward, you will also find a whole colony of sea anemones covering a huge block of coral. Here are also the classical striped clownfish, close to several black anemone fish. Swimming for a few feet over the sand bed, you can see whole fields of spotted garden eels *(Heteroconger hassi)*. These eels remain erect in the sand and sway in the current in wonderful harmony. Their tails, however, always remain in their holes. So far, no one has ever seen a single live spotted garden eel swimming freely in the water. It is impossible to observe these creatures up close; as soon as the diver approaches, they slowly but surely disappear into the sand. On the seabed, you may also often find stingrays, lying partially covered by sand.

Aquarium is a safe site for night diving, which should be avoided outside the pass. The area is rich in invertebrates that only leave their daytime hideouts after dark.

BARRACUDA POINT

BARRACUDA POINT

RANGIROA

LAGOON

N

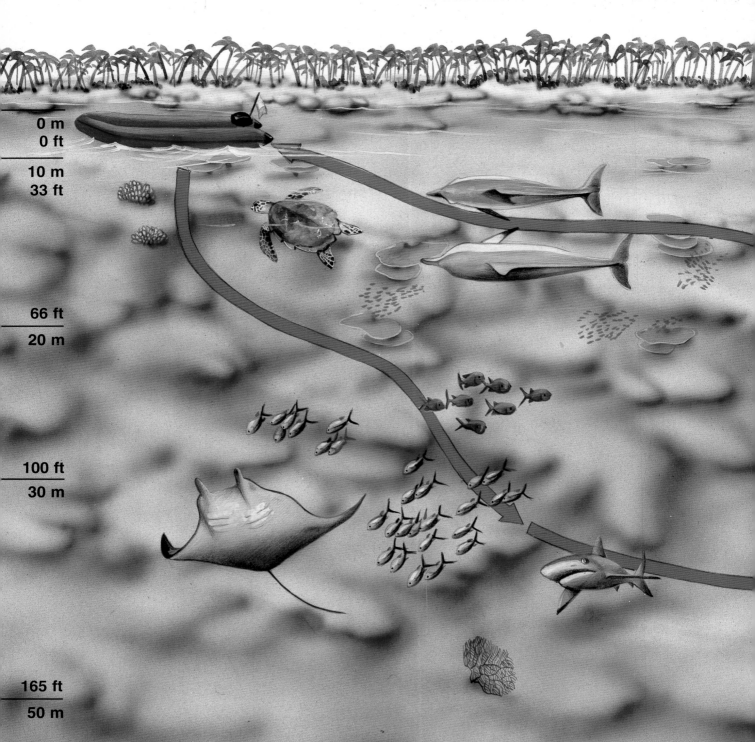

0 m
0 ft

10 m
33 ft

66 ft
20 m

100 ft
30 m

165 ft
50 m

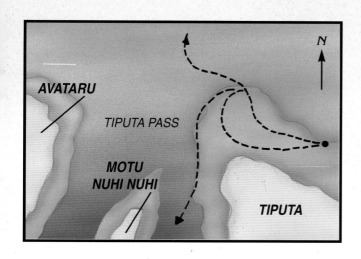

AVATARU

TIPUTA PASS

MOTU
NUHI NUHI

TIPUTA

N

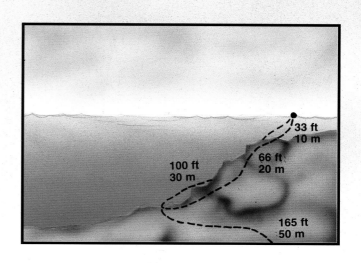

33 ft
10 m

66 ft
20 m

100 ft
30 m

165 ft
50 m

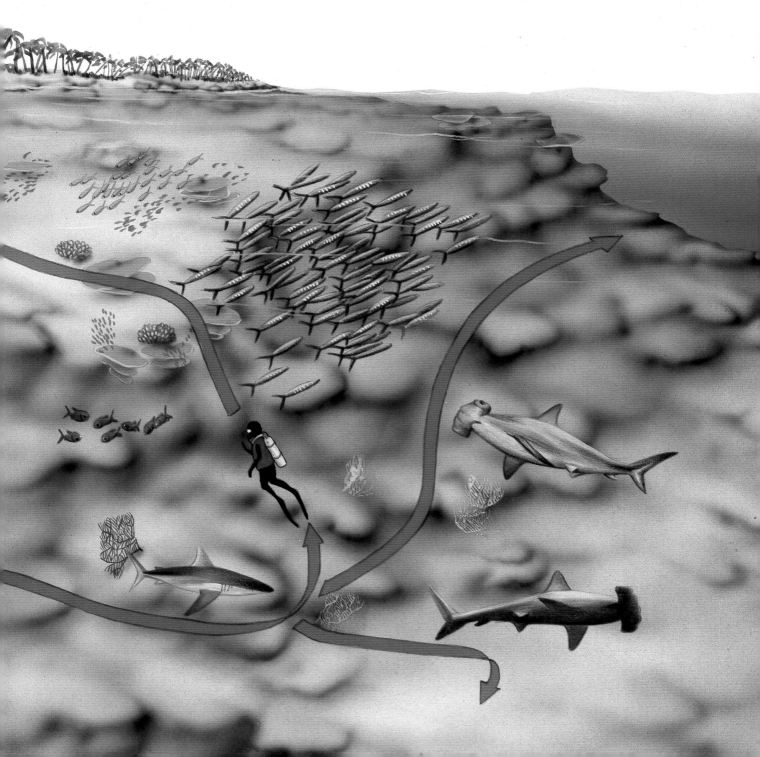

A

B

C

This dive site lies on the outer side of the reef at the mouth of the pass, just a few minutes' ride from the island on a rubber dinghy. In this region, the reef first slopes gently, then drops off in a vertical step, and finally extends into the pass. Thanks to an almost constant strong current, the area is teeming with a vast variety of underwater animals.

All dives at Barracuda Point are drift dives, in which the dive group is picked up by the rubber dinghy at the end of the trip. Divers should enter the water at the eastern end of the pass. From this point on, proceed up to the end of the pass to follow the reef and return toward the shallow plateau or head for the open waters, back toward the point where the dive started. With a qualified dive guide, it is possible to reach the lagoon in front of the village of Tiputa, following the right side of the canal as closely as possible, even going against the current.

This is a very interesting dive because on this side of the pass the reef is full of overhangs and caves teeming with an incredible number of fish. When going against the current, underwater visibility, especially in the pass, is not very good.

The best dives take advantage of an incoming tide. At these times, millions of gallons of cool seawater flow into the lagoon, bringing food. This is most certainly why so many pelagic fish, as well as dolphins, can be seen at these times in these waters. Diving possibilities in these conditions are so varied at Barracuda Point that even the most demanding divers can dive here every day for a week without getting bored. Experienced divers can follow the edge of the pass from the corner of where

D

E

the reef ends and drift with the current back into the canal, through the lagoon, and up to the islet called Motu Nuhi Nuhi. You can take another route that does not go as deep as the foot of the reef by leaving the reef to go toward the open sea. Here in the blue deep, you will find the fish that have given the place its name, a huge school of adult barracudas. They stay in compact groups in the current and often form true circles around the divers.

These waters are home to large variety of marine creatures, starting with small, colored tropical fish in the upper reaches of the reef, through to the huge pelagic creatures in the open sea and in the pass. Divers entering the water along the wall of the reef, close to the pass, are sure to encounter a school of bannerfish, soldierfish, and big-eyed perches. It is worthwhile to glance up toward the plateau of the reef from time to time because these areas are often rich in sea turtles and manta rays.

The waters at Barracuda Point, traversed by schools of mackerels and other pelagic fish, are also frequented by giant hammerhead sharks and huge manta rays from the deep. At the edge of the reef, the pass comes into view. With an incoming current, especially

during changes in moon phases, you may often come across up to fifty gray reef sharks in the current and, with luck, schools of eagle rays swimming in shallower waters. At this point, you can swim into the blue deep to observe barracudas—descending up to the center of the pass to also admire sharks and large fish—or swim back to the plateau of the reef, where you first entered the water.

The school of barracudas is naturally the high point of this dive. These schools are sometimes so huge that it is impossible to count the individual fish, which seem motionless in the current. On the way back to the reef, you will come across a large variety of exotic fish that live in the protection of the reef. The same applies when swimming along the right wall of the pass toward the lagoon; under overhangs and in caves, you may find literally thousands of reef-dwelling species.

A, G. Having explored the reef, divers venturing into the open sea are sure to encounter the barracudas that have given Barracuda Point its name.

B. Barracuda Point lies to the right of the outer corner of Tiputa Pass.

C. In the waters of the pass, one often encounters dolphins.

D. A large hammerhead shark, visiting from the deep, swims along the reef.

E. Perches parade in front of the camera.

F. Barracuda Point is famous for the large number of pelagic species to be found here. Here, a large school of blacktip sharks.

F

G

SHARK CAVE

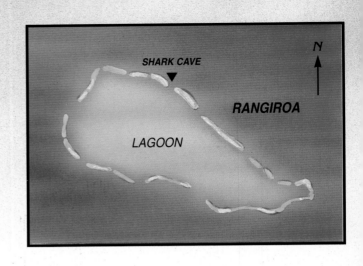

SHARK CAVE

RANGIROA

LAGOON

N

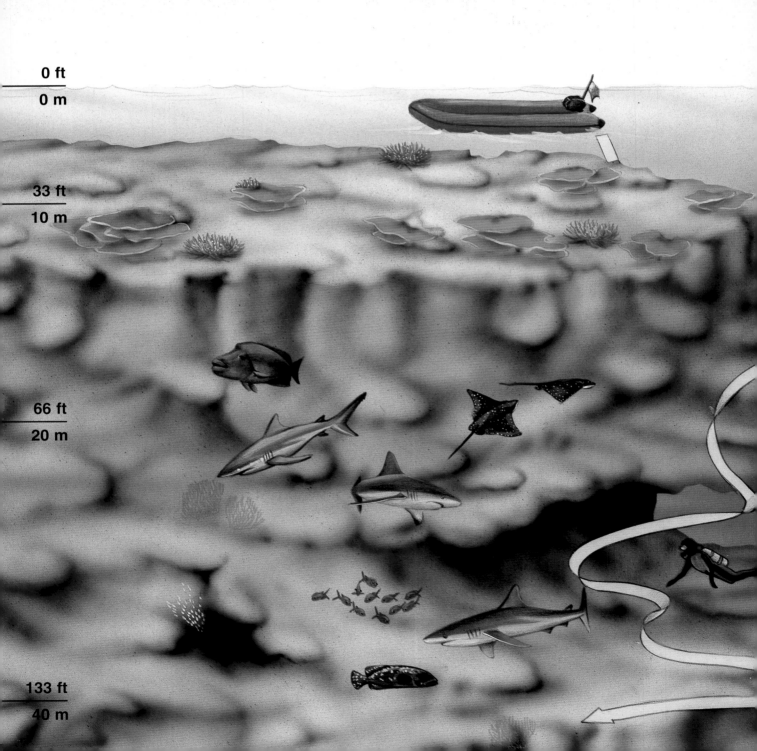

0 ft

0 m

33 ft

10 m

66 ft

20 m

133 ft

40 m

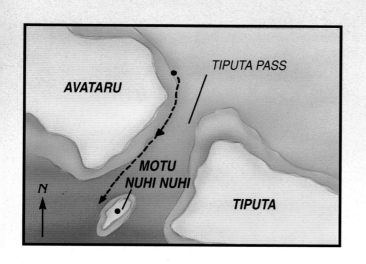

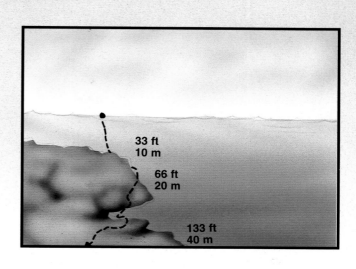

A

B

C

The dive site lies at the opening of the pass to the west, just a few minutes by dinghy from the island. The reef gradually slopes to about 33 feet (10 meters) below the surface before abruptly dropping off. At about 83 to 100 feet (25 to 30 meters) is a cave a good 65 feet (20 meters) long. At 130 feet (39 meters), the drop-off ends to extend flatly into the bed of the pass.

This dive site is only accessible during incoming tides. The site is world-famous because, especially at the full moon, it boasts a high concentration of sharks. Divers generally enter the water at a spot carefully chosen for its current. The diving party must enter the water together and then dive deep as fast as possible. With strong currents, this dive spot is accessible only to very experienced divers. In the cave itself, at a depth of about 100 feet (30 meters), there is no current at all, but the reef itself seems to have been eroded by the current, leaving no coral growth in the cave. It is therefore possible to cling to areas of the cave without doing any damage. Since this dive demands a very good familiarity with the under-water topography, dive parties must always be accompanied by a guide.

As soon as the divers enter the water, the sharks start circling around them, patrolling up and down in front

of the cave. They already know what is coming next. The divemaster has a bag full of fish, the smell of which soon attracts all of the sharks on this side of the pass. For nearly 20 minutes the sharks swim at arm's length from the divers, after which they lose interest and return to the pass. The divers can also follow the sharks into the open sea, where a current will bring them back toward the lagoon. The dive generally ends at the dive site known as Aquarium, where the boat is waiting.

The cave itself teems with soldier-fish and groupers. Napoleon wrasse appear in all sizes, swimming around inquisitively. While drift diving

through the pass, it is well worth your while to look around! In fact, with the incoming current it is quite probable to encounter a manta ray, eagle ray, or a giant hammerhead shark.

The crowd of sharks shrouds the mouth of the pass in a silvery glow. This area of the pass teems with over a hundred of these elegant predators, and the entire pass must hold many more.

The gray shark *(Carcharhinus amblyrhynchos)* has the classical characteristics of a large predator: pointed muzzle, high dorsal fin, golden eyes, and the well-known crescent-shaped mouth. Although it does not have the terrible reputation of the great white shark, it is a close cousin. The gray sharks of the South Seas are known to become aggressive in certain circumstances, but here at Rangiroa quite the opposite is true.

The gray shark can grow up to 8.5 feet (2.5 meters) in length. In the

Tiputa Pass, their average length is between 5 and 6.5 feet (1.5 and 2 meters). Shark experts believe that gray sharks are naturally social beings and that they swim in schools from a very young age. There is, however, no certain explanation for the concentration of sharks in this particular pass. A plausible reason could be that the other underwater species here provide a rich and endless source of food, or perhaps the constant current makes their lives more comfortable. Since

sharks have no gills, they must constantly swim throughout their lives to breathe.

The pass is also home to silvertip sharks *(Carcharhinus albimarginatus)*, formidable predators known as "Tapetee" by the locals. This species has a steely body made up of pure muscle and a sun-gold, shiny skin, with a shape streamlined for speed. Their behavior is much more aggressive than that of gray sharks.

A. Shark Cave in Tiputa Pass is one of the few places in the world with such a large shark population.

B. Shark Cave, an opening in the wall of Tiputa Pass at about 100 feet (30 meters) below the surface, teems with dense schools of fish, especially multi-colored perches.

C. Shark Cave is also home to a large number of groupers.

D. Sharks approach divers as soon as they enter the water. Their welcoming attitude is really due to the fact that dive guides generally feed the sharks.

E. At a depth of 100 feet (30 meters), divers can watch these awesome lords of the deep at leisure.

F. A camera flash silhouettes a silvertip shark against the blue backdrop of the deep. This species, considered potentially dangerous, lives between the surface and great depths, between 1,980 and 2,640 feet (600 and 800 meters).

MANTA POINT

MANTA POINT

N

RANGIROA

LAGOON

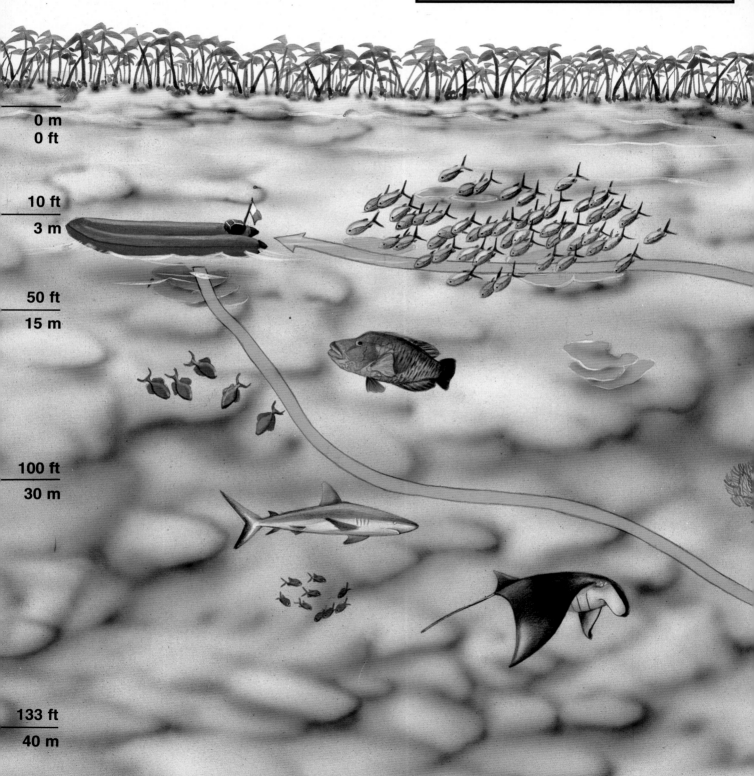

0 m
0 ft

10 ft
3 m

50 ft
15 m

100 ft
30 m

133 ft
40 m

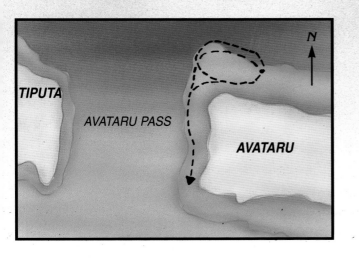

TIPUTA

AVATARU PASS

AVATARU

N

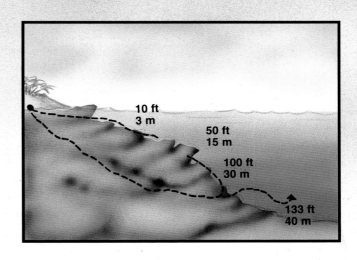

10 ft
3 m

50 ft
15 m

100 ft
30 m

133 ft
40 m

Manta Point lies on the eastern side of the Avataru Pass. An extended shallow reef stretches into the open sea from the island, close to the village of Avataru. The plateau slopes gently down to 50 feet (15 meters) and then drops steeply into the deep. The bed of the pass, 115 to 140 feet (35 to 40 meters) below the surface, is accessible to divers in both incoming and outgoing currents.

The most interesting point is the corner of the reef at the opening of the canal. However, since there is a lot to see along the way, divers generally go underwater a little more to the east. The current can only be felt in the open sea, so without an outgoing current, divers should stay close to the

reef and resurface over the platform. Divers entering the open sea in front of the reef edge will immediately see a large number of silvertip sharks (*Carcharhinus albimarginatus*). Like steel torpedoes, they come from the blue deep and swim around visitors at a safe distance before disappearing again after a few minutes.

On the reef itself, one can find all the types of reef dwellers, especially triggerfish. These 20-inch (50-centimeter)-long creatures stand on their heads on the seabed to blow away the sand and eat whatever food they uncover. With their strong jaws, they sometimes break off entire pieces of coral in their search for prey. The large dark stain that divers may see close by is really

A. Sharks crowd the waters at Manta Point, near Avataru Pass.

B. Triggerfish can be seen close to the flat areas of the reef, where they use their strange teeth to feed in a truly odd fashion: they blow on the seabed to uncover prey buried in the sand, such as sea urchins, which they then gobble up with their strong teeth.

C. Aerial view of the Avataru Pass.

D. Jacks often swim in a strange spiral formation at Manta

Point. If divers are careful not to frighten the fish, they can swim leisurely in their midst.

E. From July to September, large numbers of manta rays flock to Manta Point, attracted by the nutrient-rich waters.

F. A diver swims along the reef at Manta Point, accompanied by perches, surgeonfish, and snappers.

G. This Napoleon wrasse seems to pose for the camera.

a huge school of several hundred mackerels. If the diver approaches slowly and carefully, he can also get to the middle of the school, which revolves in a huge spiral, providing a spectacular subject for underwater photographers. One can also come across a school of surgeonfish and perhaps a few large needlefish, drifting motionless a few yards above the seabed. The reef is also home to Napoleon wrasse.

Rays also frequent these waters, especially during the summer months, when they can be seen in large shoals. The manta ray or devilfish is one of the most imposing representatives of this plankton-eating family. The fish derives its name from the two fleshy horn-shaped cephalic fins on either side of its mouth. Using these horns, the fish forms a funnel around its mouth to capture plankton as the it swims through the nutrient-rich water. Besides their odd appearance, devilfish also have the habit of jumping several feet above the water, falling back into the sea with a tremendous splash. Scientists believe that these jumps are the devilfish's attempt to rid itself of fish-lice embedded in its skin. Since they love wrapping their fleshy head fins around anchor ropes and rubbing their backs

against the hulls of ships to rid themselves of parasites, manta rays, though harmless, have been feared by seafarers and fishermen for centuries, earning them the name of "devils of the deep".

LES FAILLES

LES FAILLES LAGOON RANGIROA N

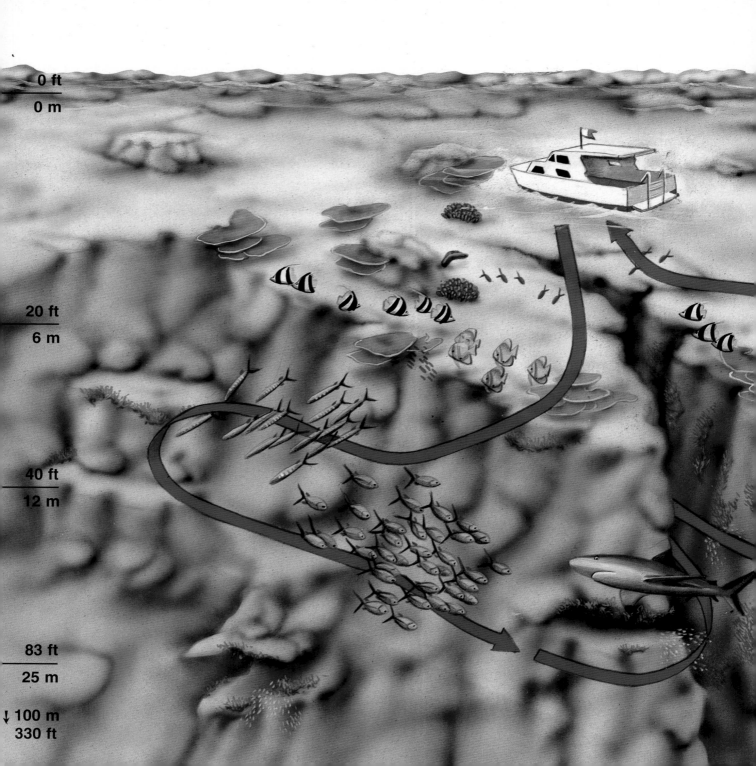

0 ft
0 m

20 ft
6 m

40 ft
12 m

83 ft
25 m

↓ 100 m
330 ft

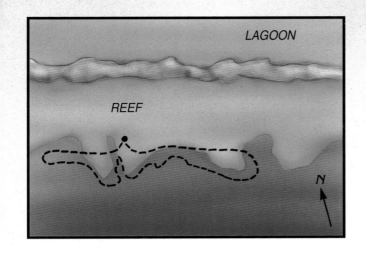

LAGOON

REEF

N

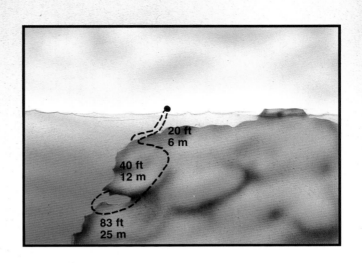

20 ft
6 m

40 ft
12 m

83 ft
25 m

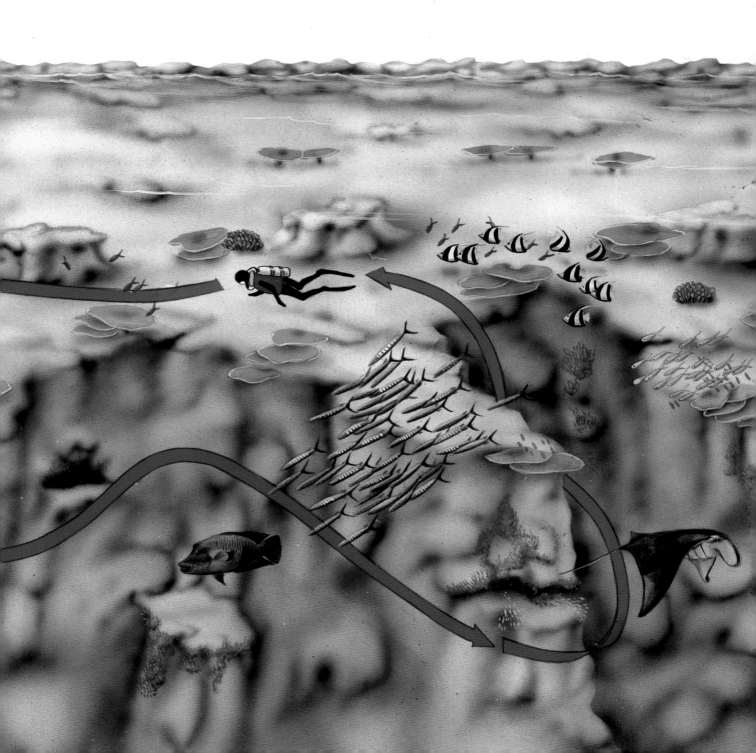

A

Les Failles lies on the west side of the Rangiroa atoll. It can be reached by crossing the lagoon diagonally, but to reach the dive spot, one must sail along the outer reef, so an excursion to this site takes an entire day. Between dives, one can also visit the Blue Lagoon. This turquoise lagoon with its lush palm vegetation is a South Sea wonder.

At the dive site, the reef abruptly falls from a depth of 20 feet (6 meters) to be lost in the great deep. But it is an underwater landscape full of ravines, caves, holes, and tunnels, covered with splendid orange hydrocorals.

Apart from onshore breezes, the area is absolutely calm and without currents. The dive starts by facing the diving

B

spot from a spur to which the boat is moored. Before starting out, settings must be carefully checked; the reef drops farther than 300 feet (91 meters).

Both sides are interesting. However, to explore the overhangs, caves and tunnels, divers should head southwest, or simply make sure that the drop-off is always to the right.

C

The orange-red glow of the coral in the cave is visible immediately after the ravine that separates the spur from the drop off. Divers are advised to carry an underwater flashlight so they can admire the vast variety of colors. Some holes under the plateau of the reef are open to sunlight, creating a fantastic atmosphere that photographers can

capture on film, using shutter speeds of 1/30 or 1/15 of a second.

From these holes, following the overhangs of the reef, you can either dive into a deep ravine that stretches up to the reef, or swim deep in a south-westerly direction along the now much less jagged walls. The clear waters at this dive site, with its spectacular underwater landscape, make it easy to forget to maintain a constant depth; keep an eye on your instruments to be sure you have sufficient air reserves left to get back to the boat at leisure. In general, it is a good idea to turn back

damaged by storms and waves. The upper regions, between 20 and 60 feet (6 and 20 meters), are inhabited by all the typical species of Pacific reef-dwelling fish. A large moray eel lives in a crevasse close to the anchorage point. While diving at Les Failles, it is worthwhile to pay close attention to the deep, since these waters are frequented by schools of pelagic fish, such as jacks and barracudas. Whitetip sharks are generally found in the upper reaches, while gray sharks live at deeper level and can often be seen swimming in groups of five to eight along the walls of the drop-off. Even sea turtles can be frequently seen here.

Manta rays and eagle rays are always present in these waters, but they are rather unpredictable, since they perpetually swim around the entire atoll ring. However, you may be lucky enough to see a school of eagle rays or giant mantas pass by.

D

when air pressure reaches 1000 psi and to select the diving depth by the amount of air consumed.

If there is still time and air, the right side of the anchorage point can also be explored. Here you will find beautiful coral formations at a depth of about 20 to 40 feet (6 to 12 meters). You can admire the orange-red corals that cover the walls, overhangs, and ceilings of the caves—hydrocorals that can only be found in a few places in Polynesia, such at the Hole in the Tikehau atoll and at Tupitipiti Point at Bora Bora.

The reef itself is covered with a lush growth of corals that are still intact here. It is worth noting that, unlike the outer reef, the reef plateau has been

A. The coral wall at Les Failles drops off to a depth of 300 (91 meters) and is full of holes and caves.

B. Aerial view of some of the motus of the coral belt around the Rangiroa Atoll.

C. The walls of Les Failles are literally carpeted with red-orange corals. These hydrocorals are generally rather rare in French Polynesia.

E

F

G

D. A diver explores one of the many underwater passages at Les Failles. Given the rather cramped space of some of these tunnels, only very experienced divers should venture into them.

E. A nurse shark seems to have dozed off in a protected area of the reef.

F. With a little luck, divers at Les Failles may also come across a few splendid manta rays as they delicately move through the water sucking in plankton.

G. In certain protected areas of the reef, one often encounters extraordinary underwater creatures, such as this sea turtle.

The Island of Tikehau

Just fifteen minutes by air west of Rangiroa lies Tikehau, a small, nearly circular atoll 17 miles (28 kilometers) in diameter. Air Tahiti runs weekly flights to the Tikehau airport, which is outside the village of Tuherahera.

Tourism has left the island quite intact so far. No luxury hotels break the idyllic beauty of the place; the atoll only features simple boarding-houses and paying guest facilities. The people of Tuherahera village are simple and warm. The local economy is based almost exclusively on fishing and copra. Until a few years ago, there was no diving at all close to the reefs of this atoll, but divers now come here from the area known as Raie Manta.

The best dive spot, as always, is the pass that provides the only link between the lagoon and the sea. Tukeiava Pass lies about 7 miles (12 kilometers) from the diving base. Diving parties generally use a swift dinghy to reach the pass. The very special site known as the Hole, about 330 yards (300 meters) to the south of Tukeiava Pass, is listed among the 100 best dive spots in the world.

A. The view shows part of the coral belt of the small atoll of Tikehau.

B. Blacktip sharks are one of the major attractions at Tikehau.

C. The waters of the lagoon of Tikehau flow into the open sea through the Tukeiava Pass.

D. Vivid corals are plentiful at the Hole, one the most famous diving sites at Tikehau.

N

A

TIKEHAU

MOTU TEONAI
▼ *Tukeiava Pass*
TUKEIAVA PASS
MOTU VAEVA
The Hole
▼
MOTU MATITI

LAGUNA

TUHERAHERA

B

C

D

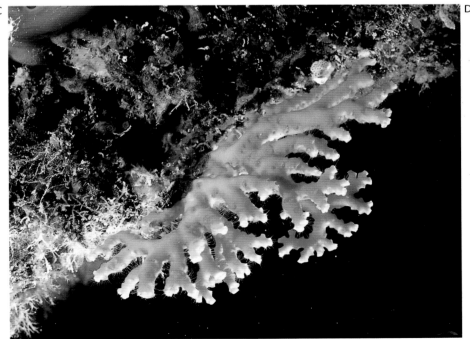

TUKEIAVA PASS

TIKEAU

TUKEIAVA PASS

LAGOON

N

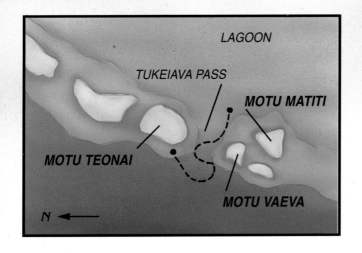

LAGOON

TUKEIAVA PASS

MOTU MATITI

MOTU TEONAI

MOTU VAEVA

N

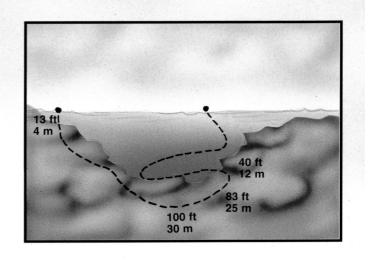

13 ftl
4 m

40 ft
12 m

83 ft
25 m

100 ft
30 m

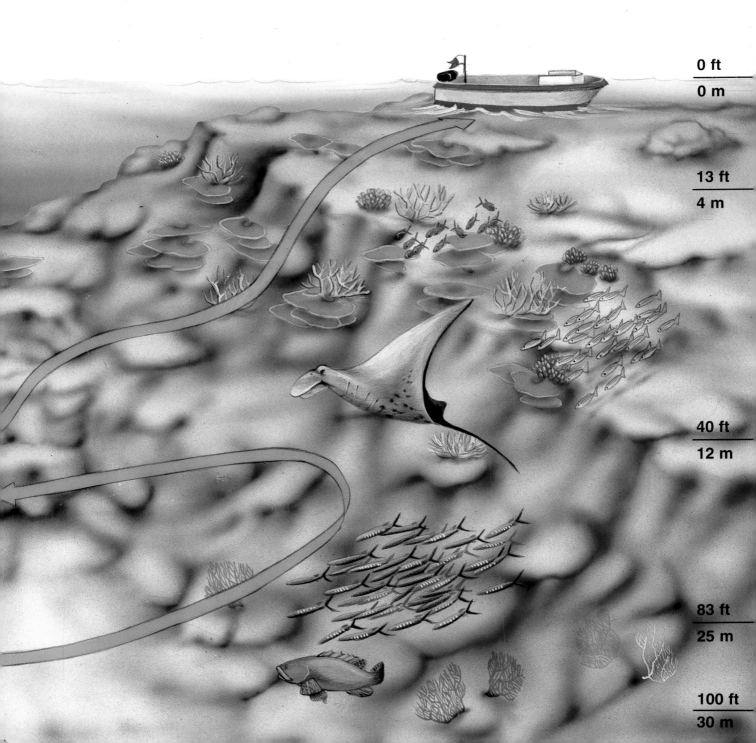

0 ft
0 m

13 ft
4 m

40 ft
12 m

83 ft
25 m

100 ft
30 m

Tukeiava Pass is the only canal that links the lagoon of the Tikehau Atoll to the ocean. The mouth of the pass faces almost north-west, and the dive site is right at the center of the canal.

Unlike the 200-foot (60-meter)-deep Tiputa Pass, this pass is rather flat, going to a depth of 115 feet (35 meters) on the side facing the sea. Toward the lagoon, the bottom lies at about 60 feet (18 meters) below the surface. Beyond the reef, that lies at a depth of 40 feet (12 meters), the pass continues up to the mouth of the lagoon at a depth of about 13 feet (4 meters).

The dive starts in front of Motu

A

B

Vaeva or Motu Teonai. From here the reef extends into the open sea, toward the mouth of the pass.

This is a drift dive. The problem at this site is timing the dive to coincide with a good incoming current. Since it is the sole pass of the atoll, and the tides are unpredictable, the dive guide can never draw up a precise dive plan in advance. However, divers can wait for good conditions right at the dive site, enjoying lunch at Motu Teonai, located directly in front of the pass.

After entering the water, divers follow the coral reef, which slopes at an angle of about 45 degrees toward the center of the pass. Divers can cross the pass along a sandy stretch at a

depth of between 82 and 100 feet (25 and 30 meters) to continue along the opposite wall of the pass. Depending on the current, you can once again cross the canal, swimming along a reef in the pass that is its most interesting point. Since the dive generally ends on the south side of the pass, the dive plan could allow for another crossing of the reef, close to the floor of the pass, where you can resurface in the shallows beyond the reef.

In optimal conditions, divers are certain to encounter spectacular marine life. Upon entering the water, close to the north side of the pass, one immediately comes across a large school of over a hundred jacks, which

looks from a distance like a huge round ball. Sharks can generally be found close to the mouth of the pass toward the open sea. Besides gray sharks, the large silvertip sharks known locally as Tapeete often swim in these waters.

This area is home to a giant grouper *(Epinephelus lanceolatus)*. These groupers are large predators that do not masticate their prey but swallow it whole, literally gulping down creatures up to one-third their size in a few seconds. The large number of small teeth that cover the jaws in several rows are only used to hold the prey. Unfortunately, our giant grouper in the Tukeiava Pass avoids the divers, and it is impossible to get a full photo of it. Interestingly, I came across the same fish during a dive in the canal and again three hours later, at the Hole, which means that the rare predator travels between these areas.

Somewhere in the middle of the pass, divers may come across a school of young barracudas swimming close to the bottom. It is worthwhile to look out into the deep and up toward the surface, to glimpse the manta rays as they go toward the ocean through the pass. As at nearly all sites in the Tikehau atoll, even here, divers are sure to encounter very large schools of soldierfish and snappers.

A. The waters of the Tukeiava Pass, the only pass of the Tikehau atoll, are frequented by extraordinary pelagic fish, such as the large silvertip shark, locally known as Tapetee.

B. A school of barracudas can often be spotted swimming above the sandy bottom of the pass.

C. During the dive, especially from the bottom of the pass, divers should look up to catch a glimpse of a manta ray, accompanied by pilotfish, heading out into the ocean.

D. The Tukeiava Pass is also home to a dense school of jacks.

E. Countless schools of multicolored fish, such as these striped snappers, swim in the waters behind the reef of the Tukeiava Pass.

F. A large moray eel peeks out of its den in a coral formation close to the bottom of the pass.

G. Close-up of the strange snout of a triggerfish.

C

D

E

F

G

THE HOLE

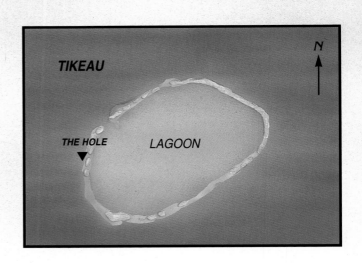

TIKEAU

THE HOLE ◢ LAGOON

N

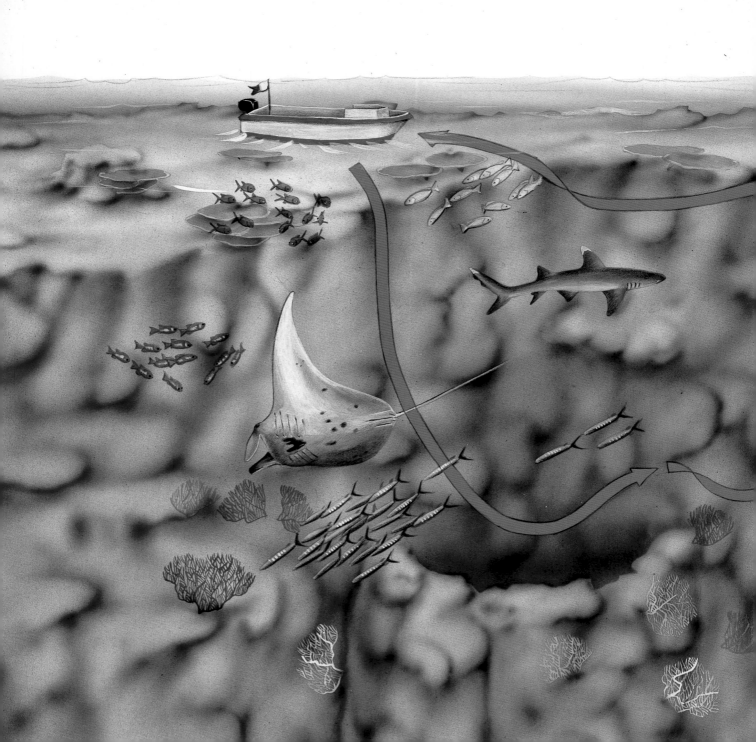

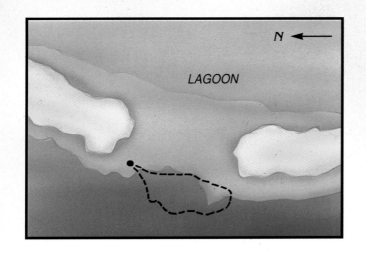

LAGOON

N ←

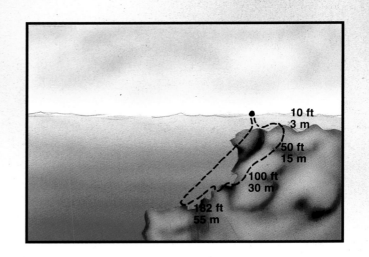

10 ft
3 m

50 ft
15 m

100 ft
30 m

182 ft
55 m

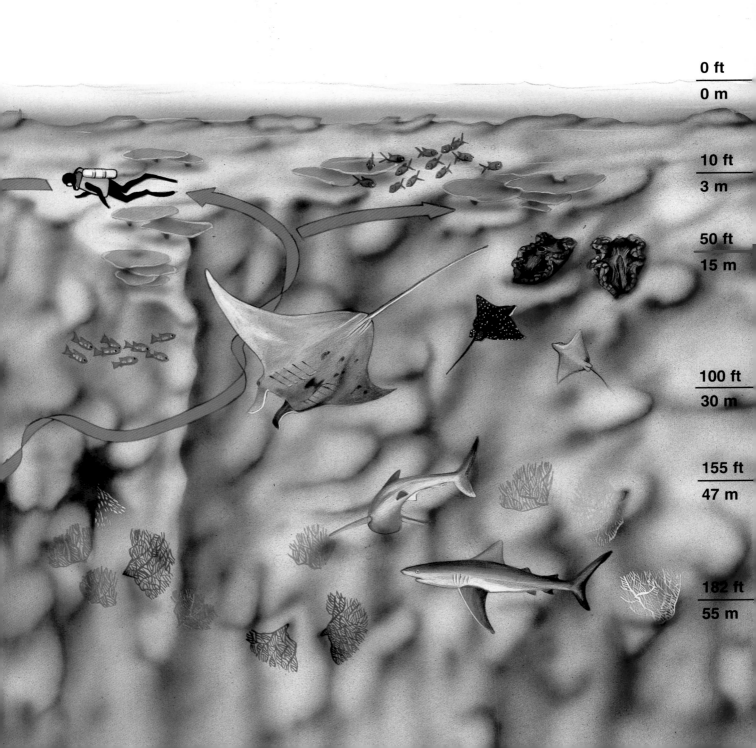

0 ft

0 m

10 ft

3 m

50 ft

15 m

100 ft

30 m

155 ft

47 m

182 ft

55 m

Like all the other diving spots at Tikehau, the Hole is close to the Tukeiava Pass. The spot is not marked, and only a rather prominent rock on the coast indicates its approximate position. The dive guide accompanying the divers generally leads them to the right entry point, according to the current and waves, so that they can easily find the Hole. The bulge in the nearly straight reef edge is clearly visible for quite a distance. The summit of the reef lies only 10 to 13 feet (3 to 4 meters) underwater, and the drop-off starts at a depth of about 30 feet (9 meters), after which the wall falls abruptly into the deep.

Since the area forms a sort of creek in the reef, one gets the feeling that one is diving through a funnel that ends lower in the Hole. The black opening, which can inspire a feeling of danger, is about 33 feet (10 meters) in diameter and forms a vertical tunnel that goes very deep to join the outer reef. The same applies to a smaller canal that, seen from the sea toward the reef, starts on the right. The two tunnels end at about 265 feet (80 meters), nearly at the foot of the outer reef. The currents that flow in and out through these tunnels are the reason for the huge wealth of underwater life and coral growth at the Hole. Unfortunately the tunnels go too deep to allow for

D

A. The clear waters of the Tukeiava Pass, facing the Hole, allow for excellent photographs, such as this school of yellowtail snapper, with a diver against the turquoise blue background of the water.

B. A dense school of red perches often swims close to the reef.

C. The walls of the Hole are famous for their dense encrustation of brightly colored coral.

diving without a special mixtures of gas. But even the spectacular view from the bottom toward the surface makes diving here an unforgettable experience.

At this point, the boat does not stop, but allows the divers to enter the water in the open sea. Following the classical dive plan, the divers immediately descend. Even from above the Hole, the view is impressive. Naturally it is not advisable to remain here very long, and you must move on to the left or right along the reef. Time and air allowing, the dive trip can continue close to the edge of the reef or on the plateau. Depending on the wind and the weather, the waves can be quite strong, since the surface of the reef is not very far underwater. Any safety stops must be done in the open sea, while enjoying the extraordinary wealth of these waters. Even on the edge of the reef, divers will come across large numbers of soldierfish and snappers, in huge schools that swarm by the wall of the reef like a red cloud going up to 100 feet (30 meters) in depth. Photographers will not be disappointed here; the area affords spectacular pictures. Nearby there is always a school of sea barbels close to the slope of the reef, and a school of hundreds of big-eyed perches lives at the south side. Coral growth is varied

and intact. Many of the corals extend far into the open sea, and large snappers can be seen all over the place. Below a depth of about 100 feet (30 meters), one comes across orange-red sea fans, as well as a purple variety. Groupers are common, and it is not rare to see large moray eels peeking from the openings in the walls. Depending on the current, you may also come across many gray sharks swimming around in circles at the entrance to the Hole. The conditions here make for an excellent hunting ground for schools of mackerels and other predators of the open sea. Here one can in fact always find sharks; if not in the hole, then at the northern end or coming up

D. These corals, arranged in an orderly pattern, seem to flourish at a depth of 100 feet (30 meters).

E. Around the mouth of the hole that gives the site its name, you may encounter a large number of predators, such as this threatening-looking gray shark.

F. Jacks are plentiful at the Hole and often swim in schools so compact that they seem like balls.

E

F

from the blue depths as the divers end their trip over the reef. As with all diving trips to outer reefs, it is well worth your while to pay some attention to the open sea. Only then can you see eagle rays gliding majestically past, or observe manta rays as they swim near the reef.

The Island of Manihi

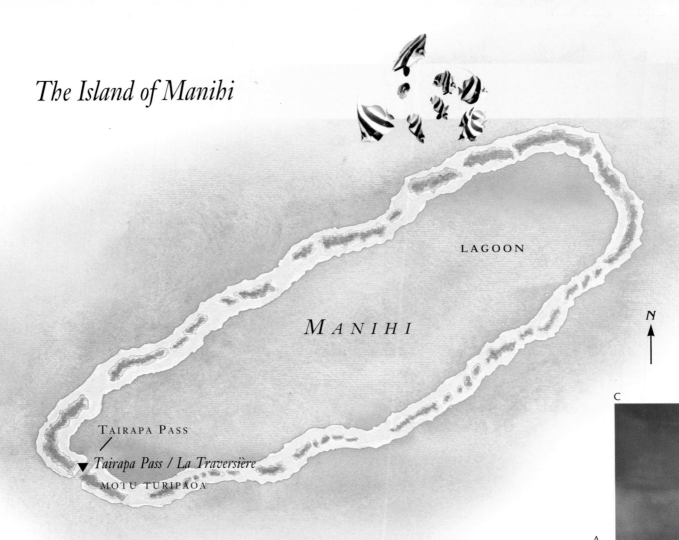

LAGOON

MANIHI

TAIRAPA PASS

Tairapa Pass / La Traversière

MOTU TURIPAOA

N

A fter Rangiroa, Manihi is the second most visited atoll of the Tuamotu Archipelago. The main attraction here is the white sand beach. The lagoon is very small, just 6 miles (10 kilometers) wide and 12 miles (20 kilometers) long. From the island, therefore, the entire lagoon can be admired in the full beauty of all its colors.

The more or less fifty houses of the village of Turipaoa share a sand beach that leads from the airport to the lagoon. Manihi is served daily by Air Tahiti's twin-engined aircraft. Access to the village from the airport is by sea. Besides its beaches, Manihi's sources of income also include a large pearl farm.

The island is an underwater paradise, with excellent dive sites, the best of which are at the Tairapa Pass at the western end of the atoll.

Diving in the reef cuts depends on the currents, and drift diving can also be done here.

A

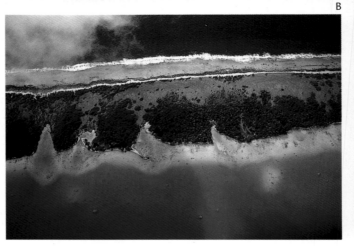

B

C

A, B. The spectacular colors of the lagoon and the coral belt of the Manihi atoll.

C. Looking over almost the entire atoll of Manihi, 12 miles (20 kilometers) long and 6 miles (10 kilometers) wide.

D. The most frequented dive sites at Manihi are close to the Tairapa Pass.

E. The waters off the Tuamotu Archipelago are inhabited by an incredible wealth of marine life, such as this butterflyfish, intent on eating coral polyps.

D

E

TAIRAPA PASS

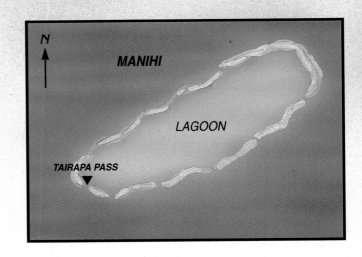

MANIHI

LAGOON

N

TAIRAPA PASS

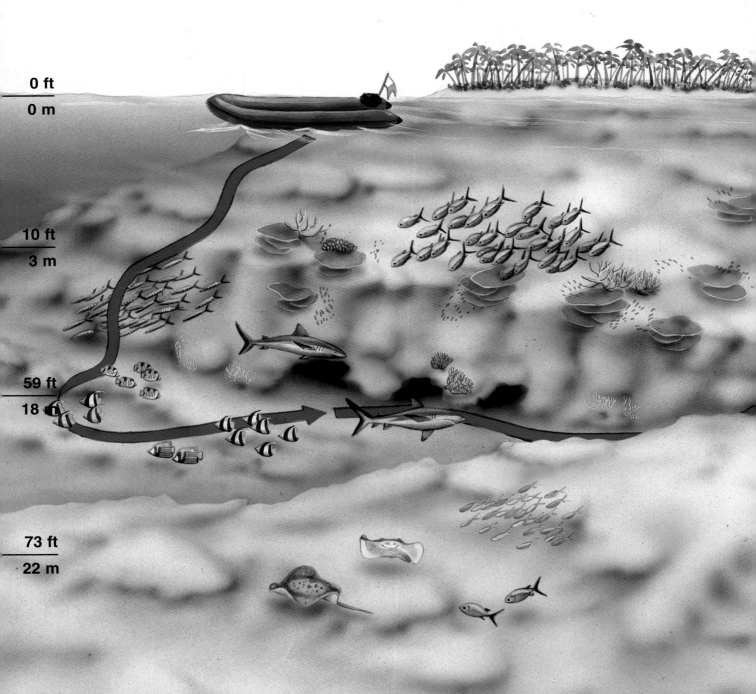

0 ft
0 m

10 ft
3 m

59 ft
18 m

73 ft
22 m

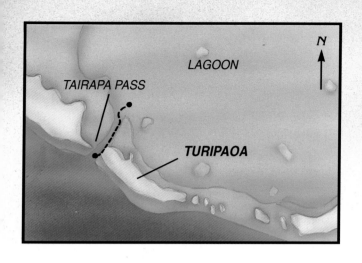

LAGOON

N

TAIRAPA PASS

TURIPAOA

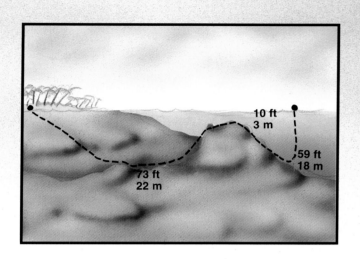

10 ft
3 m

73 ft
22 m

59 ft
18 m

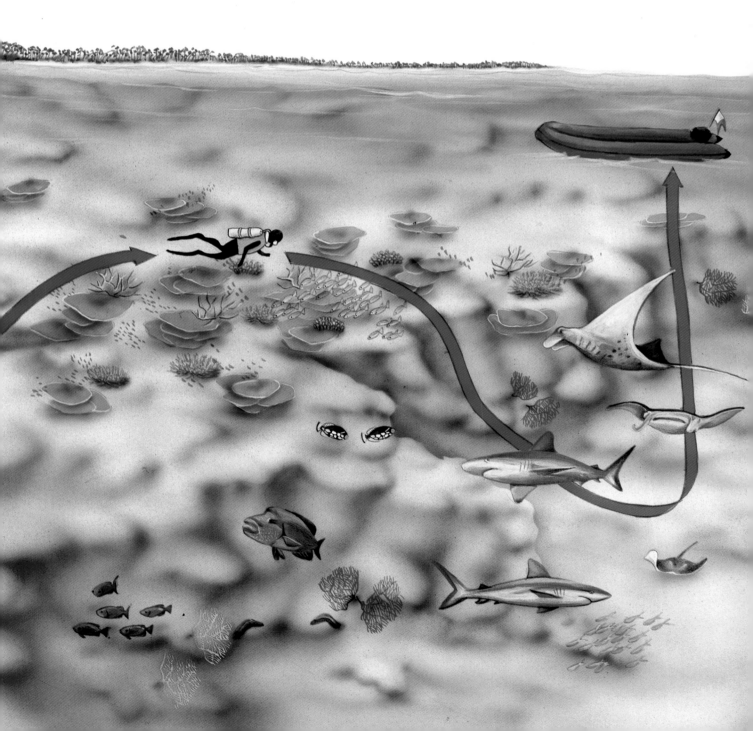

A

Tairapa Pass is the only link between the Manihi lagoon and the sea. The currents are very strong and rich in nutrients, attracting a large number of fish, to the great joy of divers. While the pass is easily accessible, it features extraordinary marine life. Located on a southwest-northeast axis, the corridor of the pass extends for 440 yards (400 meters), with a breadth of 165 feet (50 meters) and a depth of 65 feet (20 meters), making it a huge aquarium. The pass can be crossed from end to end without a single armstroke. Divers are carried by the current, but stop from time to

B

time along the way. At the end of the dive they are picked up the surface vessel.

At and around Tairapa are about ten dive sites that are well worth exploring. The dive starts at the entry

C

to the pass on the western side in front of the village. The incoming current bears very clear water. After a quick dive into the water, the divers are suspended at a depth of 50 to 65 feet (15 to 20 meters). Visibility is excellent;

A. Tairapa Pass includes a true aquarium in the open sea: the picture shows a large shoal of vermilion perches.

B. View of Tairapa Pass, the only breach in the Manihi atoll.

C. A diver gets a close-up view of a large manta ray as it elegantly glides by.

D. The reef of Tairapa Pass is also home to a few groupers, like the three here.

E, F. It's worth the time to examine the seabed, which often hides creatures such as these shy stingrays (E) and timid ballfish (F).

G. Several butterfly-fish swim around the reef in search of food.

protected resting places for sharks. A little lower, honeycomb stingrays disturb the sand as they forage for food. Both sides of the pass feature a parade of strangely named fish: emperor angelfish, porcupinefish, balloonfish, boxfish, dragonfish, trumpetfish, and so on.

At a depth of about 83 feet (25 meters) a wall blocks the passage between the two main walls of the pass corridor. The current flows around the obstacle, the rising flux of water carrying the divers to about 17 feet (5 meters) below the surface. As the seabed slowly slopes upward, the current increases in intensity, and the divers are borne along the reef without ever touching it—an enchanting experience. Jacks in close formation swim like torpedoes against the current. The bottom rises farther, up to 10 feet (3 meters) below the surface, and the current picks up even more speed as it passes the crest and sweeps the divers into the lagoon. This thrilling drift dive lasts no more than three minutes. While the divers slowly regain their balance in the calm waters of the lagoon, the waters at the surface, bubbling in the turbulence caused by the strong current, seem to explode in spray.

The current can hardly be felt in the lagoon, and the filtered sunlight is less blue, draping the landscape in a lunar atmosphere. These waters, rich in triggerfish, Napoleon wrasse, and blacktip sharks, are above all a meeting place for manta rays, which swim majestically in front of the divers, pretending to leave, only to come even closer. During most of the year the group is only made up of three or four

the bottom, 17 feet (5 meters) below, and the walls on each side, as well as the keel of the surface vessel, are all clearly visible. Divers can calmly enjoy the sight of moray eels, triggerfish, sole, parrotfish, fluorescent blue shoals of perches, schools of barracuda, and jacks in small formations, as well as schools of butterflyfish swimming against the current—the list could go on endlessly. A little ahead, at the foot of the wall, lies the mouth of a cave, in front of which a group of whitetip sharks (Triaenodon obesus) basks motionless close to the bottom, facing the current. Some of these caves offer

members, but in July and August manta rays congregate in great numbers, regaling divers with a spectacular underwater ballet, their antics reminiscent of acrobatic air shows.

LA TRAVERSIÈRE

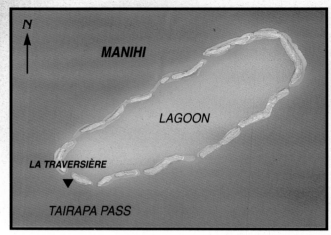

MANIHI

LAGOON

LA TRAVERSIÈRE

TAIRAPA PASS

0 m
0 ft

3 m
10 ft

66 ft
20 m

96 ft
29 m

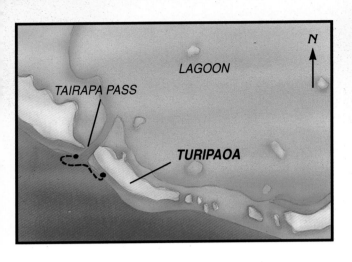

LAGOON

N

TAIRAPA PASS

TURIPAOA

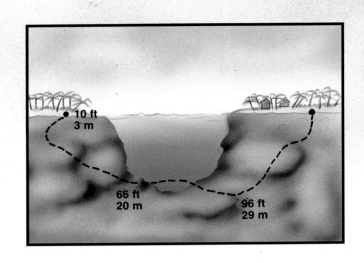

10 ft
3 m

66 ft
20 m

96 ft
29 m

A

The mouth of Tairapa Pass, La Traversière, which opens onto the ocean south-southeast, is thus protected from the strong winds that blow east-northeast most of the year. Since this natural canal is relatively narrow, it can be crossed from end to end at a medium depth underwater, on the side facing the ocean, which features a magnificent drop-off descending thousands of feet. Two surface buoys indicate the points of immersion and resurfacing. Dives are at varying depths depending on the changing underwater landscape, in an area featuring alternate incoming and outgoing currents and thus diverse underwater fauna.

Dives generally are timed for an outgoing current, and include exploration of the drop-off and the two plateaus above it.

We begin at the buoy close to the village, on the coral platform, descending into very clear water. The area is full of fish—several schools of surgeonfish, blue and green parrotfish, angelfish, butterflyfish, and yellow-headed triggerfish. At a depth of 10 feet (3 meters), we reach the nearby drop-off and descend gradually to the right, toward the pass. The drop-off is very rich in life, and it is worth an entire dive on its own, with its schools of perches, holes full of mullets,

whitetip sharks *(Triaenodon obesus)*, blue mackerel, and scorpionfish. A glance at the deep can reveal a hundred barracudas in tight formation or a passing flight of honeycomb stingrays.

After about ten minutes at a depth of 83 to 100 feet (25 to 30 meters), the corner of the pass comes into view. You begin to feel the outgoing current, and the beautiful blue of the ocean gives way to water full of nutrients from the lagoon. The landscape forms a huge slope facing the ocean. The incline is not very steep, and it is better to move close to the bed, using your hands from time to time. The outgoing current is easily visible several feet overhead.

B

C

D

Crossing the pass takes a few minutes at a depth of about 65 feet (20 meters). The dive guide generally pauses during the crossing, since the underwater spectacle is breathtaking. The topography causes regular turbulence in midcurrent, attracting splendid schools of barracudas and,

E

more rarely, one or two manta rays that seem to float motionless in the current. Closer to the bottom, one regularly encounters a few Napoleon wrasse and giant boxfish. Farther below, large coral formations shelter loaches and giant moray eels.

At the other end of the mouth of the pass, you once again find the beautiful blue of the ocean and the light of the drop-off, so dear to photographers. If the species on this side are more or less the same, you cannot help noticing that here they form denser schools: yellow perches, paddle perches, big-eyed mackerels, and sometimes a good dozen sharks.

Lastly, after a pleasant swim along the drop-off, the dive ends in 10 feet (3 meters) of water on the coral platform, generally amid a splendid school of surgeonfish.

Each year, at the beginning of July, for about 2 to 3 weeks, Tairapa Pass is the scene of a huge assembly of loaches. This is the mating period, and tens of thousands of these loaches invade the surroundings of the pass. This can also be seen in other atolls of the Tuamotu Archipelago, but it is probably easiest to observe it here.

A. In the sandy stretches on the bottom of Tairapa Pass, one comes across large ballfish.

B. The waters of the pass are often frequented by large manta rays, swimming in the nutrient-rich current.

C. A large number of tropical fish can be found along the walls of the reef, such as these striped snappers accompanied by a large grouper.

D. The pale sand in the pass bears the shadow of a whitetip reef shark.

E. Shoals of perches are a highlight of diving the Tairapa Pass.

F, G. La Traversière, where divers can explore both sides of the pass. On the bottom, divers will also come across a large number of pelagic fish, such as this group of eagle rays (F) or a shoal of slender barracuda (G).

THE MARQUESAS ISLANDS

Indian Rock ▼

ILE DE SABLE

HATUATUA

EIAO

MOTU ITI

NUKU HIVA

Stingray Cave ▼ *Tikapo Rock*

Matateiko Point ▼

Motumano Point

UA POU

T he Marquesas Islands, the northernmost archipelago of French Polynesia, are situated at about 1,400 miles from Tahiti. The archipelago was forced to the surface of the sea by violent underwater volcanic eruptions, and today they contrast with the sky as mute witnesses to the past. The islands are the perfect paradise for all of those who love unspoiled, wild, rough landscape, with steep rocks, mountain peaks, and valleys. The Marquesas radiate an indescribable fascination, reflected in the books of Herman Melville, the songs of Jacques Brel, and the paintings of Paul Gauguin. Brel and Gauguin wanted to make the islands their permanent home, and both are buried on the island of Hiva Oa.

The Marquesas could be considered the very end of the earth. This feeling seemed to be with me always as I sailed through these islands, since for days we did not spot a single other human on land or at sea.

These islands are also striking for their uncommonly diverse vegetation,

not found in any other archipelago. Another symbol of the area is surely the presence, side by side with indigenous animals, of many wild oxen, goats, and horses, brought here over a hundred years ago by a Chilean bishop. The islands abound in bananas, mangoes, and papayas, while the coastal sea provides the best seafood and crustaceans.

The overall land area is about 806 square miles (1,300 square kilometers), and Nuku Hiva, the largest island, with its 205 square miles (330 square kilometers), is seconded by ten other islands. The lack of previously formed coral reefs has resulted in the near total absence of flat beaches. Steep cliffs rise abruptly from the sea. The entire network of road links between villages follows mountain crests and valleys. Traveling here is difficult, requiring cross-country vehicles, and even then, during heavy rains, the trip may become a rather dangerous adventure. It is much easier to go from one end of the island to the other by boat. Even in this case, however, the

islanders are at the mercy of the weather, since the sea can become as wild as the land. For several days a year, it is impossible to travel along these storm-beaten coastlines.

HISTORY

The archipelago was formerly known by the Polynesians as the "Land of Men." In 1595, the Spaniard Alvaro de Mendaña became the first European to land on these islands, and he named them Las Marquesas de Mendoza in honor of the Spanish viceroy.

The discovery of the islands was kept secret for as long as possible to prevent their falling into the hands of England, then the archenemy of Spain. The arrival of the Spaniards marked the most bloody and shameful period of exploration in the South Seas by Westerners. The proud and savage islanders used all their means and power to resist, until 95 percent of them were killed. Of the 100,000 islanders that peopled the archipelago at the outset of the exploration, only 15,000 were left in 1842 when the French "protectors" arrived; in 1926 this number fell to 2,000.

Today the islands have a population of 7,500. Since they are so remote, the Marquesas have been largely neglected until now.

DIVING

Although there are weekly air links between Tahiti and Nuku Hiva and the neighboring Hiva Oa Island, this Pacific archipelago will never become a mass tourist destination. It will always be a paradise for nature lovers, offering endless challenges to divers in the strangest undersea landscapes, populated by the most incomparable fish.

Although the waters here are not rich in coral forests as in the Tuamotu Islands, they offer a huge range of underwater life. Coastal areas abound in spectacular manta rays and hammerhead sharks. A meeting with the melonhead whales that swim in huge schools around the island is an unforgettable experience. These waters,

the richest in fish in the whole of Polynesia, are also home to certain rare endemic species.

Diving is nearly always done from a large seaworthy boat, directly at the foot of the high, eroded sea cliffs or over offshore reefs. Visitors must always remember that visibility can change sharply with the current; the crystal-clear water of the Tuamotu Islands is absent here. Sailing through the Marquesas Island is a special thrill. Cruises on modern catamarans, lasting several days, allow visitors to dive off the remote and uninhabited islands of Eiao and Hatutu.

C

D

E

A, B. Nuku Hiva, in the Marquesas archipelago, is a volcanic island covered by dense vegetation.

C. Melonhead whales, found in large groups in the Marquesas.

D. Rays are the main attraction at Stingray Cave, Nuku Hiva.

E. The waters of the Marquesas, rich in plankton and micro-organisms, attract many schools of fish, like this dense shoal of jacks.

UA UKA

FATU HUKU

HIVAOA

MOTANE

TAHUATA

FATU HIVA

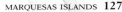

The Island of Nuku Hiva

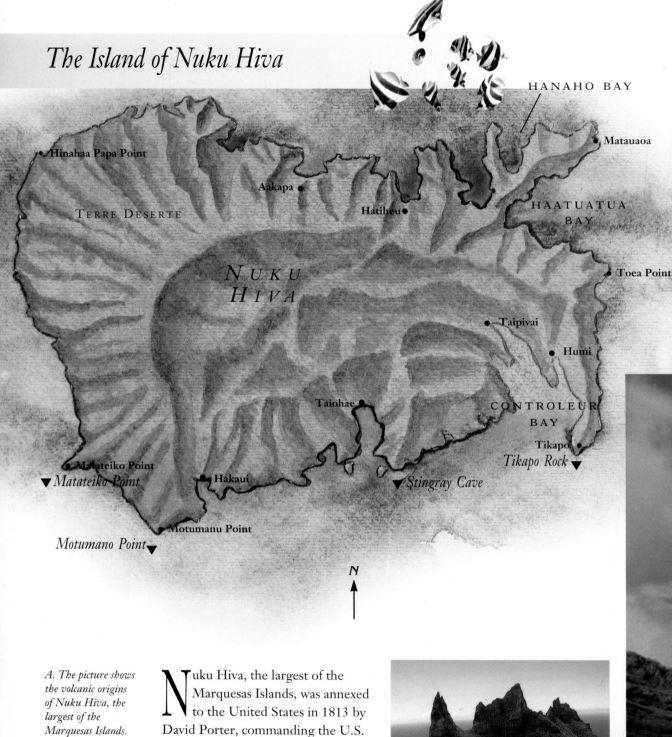

HANAHO BAY

Matauaoa

HAATUATUA BAY

Toea Point

Hinahaa Papa Point

Aakapa

TERRE DESERTE

Hatiheu

NUKU HIVA

Taipivai

Humi

Taiohae

CONTROLEUR BAY

Tikapo
Tikapo Rock ▼

▼ *Matateiko Point*
Matateiko Point

Hakaui

Stingray Cave

Motumanu Point

Motumano Point ▼

N

A. The picture shows the volcanic origins of Nuku Hiva, the largest of the Marquesas Islands. The island has a very uneven surface, and is in some areas totally inaccessible. The highest point on the island, Mount Takao, reaches 4,039 feet (1,224 meters).

B. A catamaran skirts the steep and hostile north coast of Nuku Hiva, close to Haatuatua Bay.

Nuku Hiva, the largest of the Marquesas Islands, was annexed to the United States in 1813 by David Porter, commanding the U.S. warship *Essex*. At the point now known as Taiohae, he built a fort that he baptized Madisonville in honor of the U.S. president. Nothing remains today of this fort or of other forts built later by the French. While the island was an American colony, Herman Melville set his novel *Typee* on this island. The novel, now considered a classic, describes life on the Marquesas in the nineteenth century.

Mount Takao rises in the center of the island to reach 4,039 feet (1,224

A

meters) in height. Nuku Hiva is very mountainous, and certain areas are inaccessible. The island is served only by a single, rather badly maintained road, which cannot be used for a long time after heavy rains. The few vehicles on the island are therefore all four-wheel-drive. However, a helicopter service has been set up to serve tourists.

B

C. The seabed and waters off the Marquesas Islands are home to an extraordinary variety of marine life, sometimes very different from that found elsewhere in Polynesia. Here, a delicate anemone with very fine tentacles is painted in muted colors.

D. A yellow-edged moray (Gymnothorax flavimarginatus) peeks out of his den, the walls of which are covered with amazing marine creatures, such as cleaner prawns—recognizable by their long antennae—encrusting sponges, and brightly colored corals.

TIKAPO ROCK

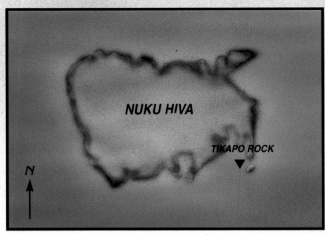

NUKU HIVA

TIKAPO ROCK

N

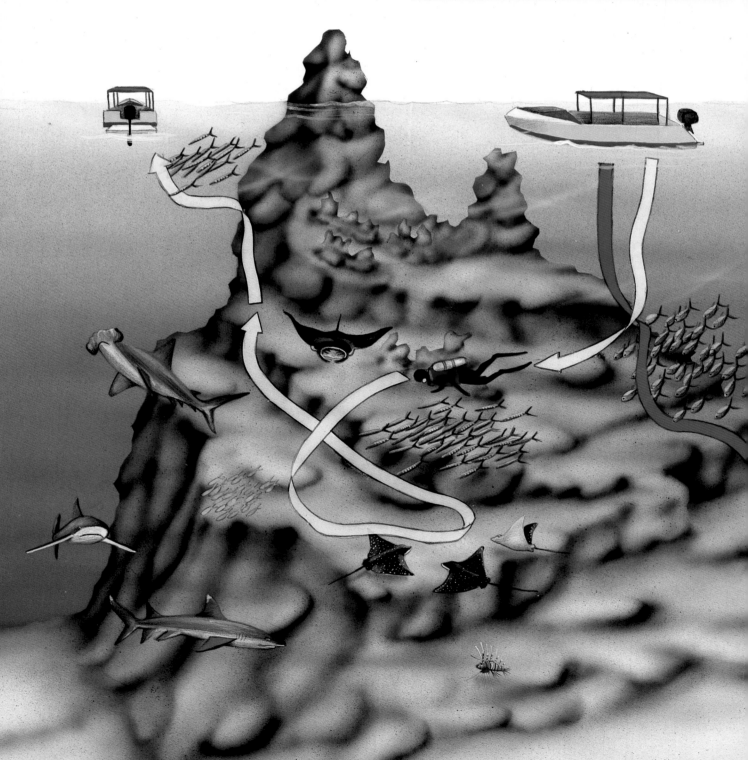

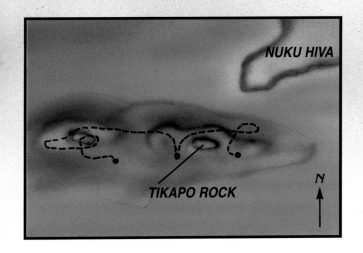

NUKU HIVA

TIKAPO ROCK

N

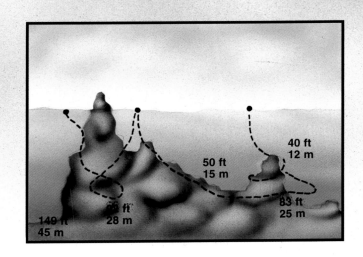

149 ft
45 m

68 ft
28 m

50 ft
15 m

40 ft
12 m

83 ft
25 m

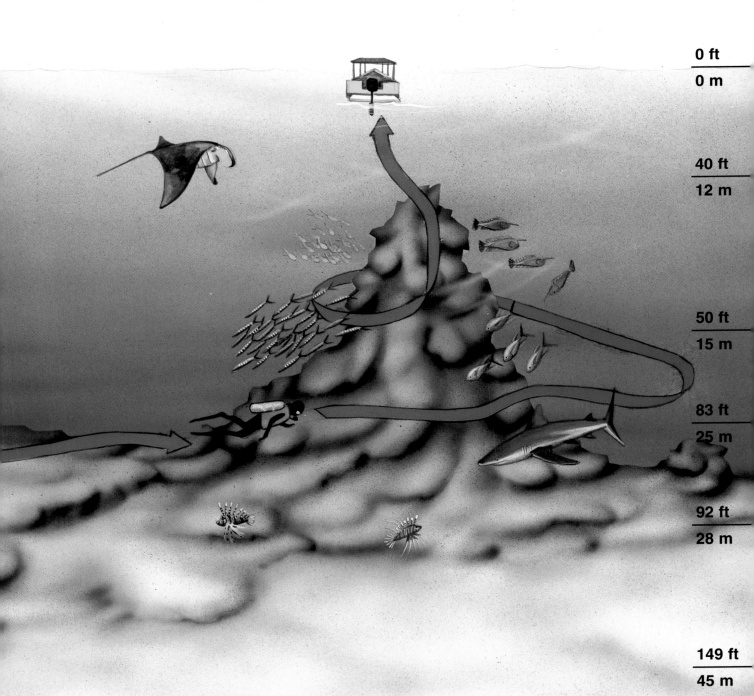

0 ft
0 m

40 ft
12 m

50 ft
15 m

83 ft
25 m

92 ft
28 m

149 ft
45 m

A

B

C

Tikapo Rock is on the south coast of the Nuku Hiva island. The tip of the rock rises abruptly from the sea, about 330 yards (300 meters) off the coast. The area above the surface of the water is in truth only the smallest part of the coral reef that extends from east to west. The reef remains unparalleled in landscape and marine life.

Ideal diving conditions here are found when there is no north or west wind. However, even with a west wind, divers can swim underwater, using only their breathing equipment, to the east coast to observe huge, breathtaking schools of melonhead whales. Divers generally leave the boat close to the rock so as to better see the reef and reach it with ease. This area can be visited in several ways, but the waiting point of the boat must be well planned in advance. One can either go around the rock rising from the water or follow the rocky hump eastwards, where there is another peak, quite like the Matterhorn in the Alps, but underwater, at a depth of about 40 feet (12 meters). Following this diving plan, divers resurface at a point marked by marker buoys. This plan provides for a spectacular dive, because most of the marine life lies between the two rocky peaks. This dive plan must, however, be avoided during strong currents. This area is also teeming with fish, especially in areas exposed to the current.

The large numbers of ledges and platforms at the bottom allow for a great variety of diving styles. Tikapo Rock gives visitors nearly everything that the Marquesas have to offer in terms of underwater life. Those in search of large fish will find schools of jacks and barracudas to the east of the rock. Depending on the current, one can come across eagle rays, which remain immobile in the water despite very strong currents. You may find the rare silky sharks here, as well as

to come to the very limits of its safety distance, which provides for excellent observation but is still too far for good photographs.

This fissured landscape, full of countless caves, cracks and holes, includes all the species of the scorpionfish family, which hover like multicolored and

E

D. The camera lens captures a few snapper, numerous around the coral walls at Tikapo Rock.

E. The waters of the Marquesas Islands are inhabited by a large number of endemic species, such as this unique moray eel.

F. A scorpionfish, perhaps fleeing from the photographer, extends its winglike fins to rise elegantly above the reef.

D

F

A. During the descent along the reef of Tikapo Rock, divers will come across a variety of soft corals. A good light is necessary to admire the delicate pastel hues of these coelenterates, in the darker areas underwater.

B. The picture shows the rich underwater life at Tikapo Rock.

C. The waters of Tikapo Rock attract a large number of various kinds of sharks. In the picture, the unmistakable outline of a silvertip reef shark.

scalloped hammerhead sharks, which are quite common in these waters, and gray or whitetip reef sharks. Divers here must bear in mind that other inhabitants of the sea can come up from the endless blue deep at any time. Since visibility is generally at an average of 65 feet (20 meters), these unexpected encounters are a real thrill. Everywhere in this area, the seabed is of volcanic rock, richly carpeted by soft and hard corals, sponges, and calcium-rich seaweed in a wide variety of colors, though the magnificent lilac and purple tones become visible only with the use of a light or camera strobe. A huge grouper between or over rocks may allow divers

exotic birds above the seabed. These fish have large side fins that resemble the wings of a bird, allowing them to move in the water in rapid darts. They are also poisonous, and dangerous to man. To protect both the marine environment and themselves, divers must be careful to avoid touching anything, even the seabed.

The west side of the large rock is a paradise for moray eels. At a depth of 13 to 33 feet (4 to 10 meters), the reef is full of holes and cracks that are home to hydrocoral and various morays of the yellow-edged variety (*Gymnothorax flavimarginatus*).

STINGRAY CAVE

NUKU HIVA

STINGRAY CAVE

N

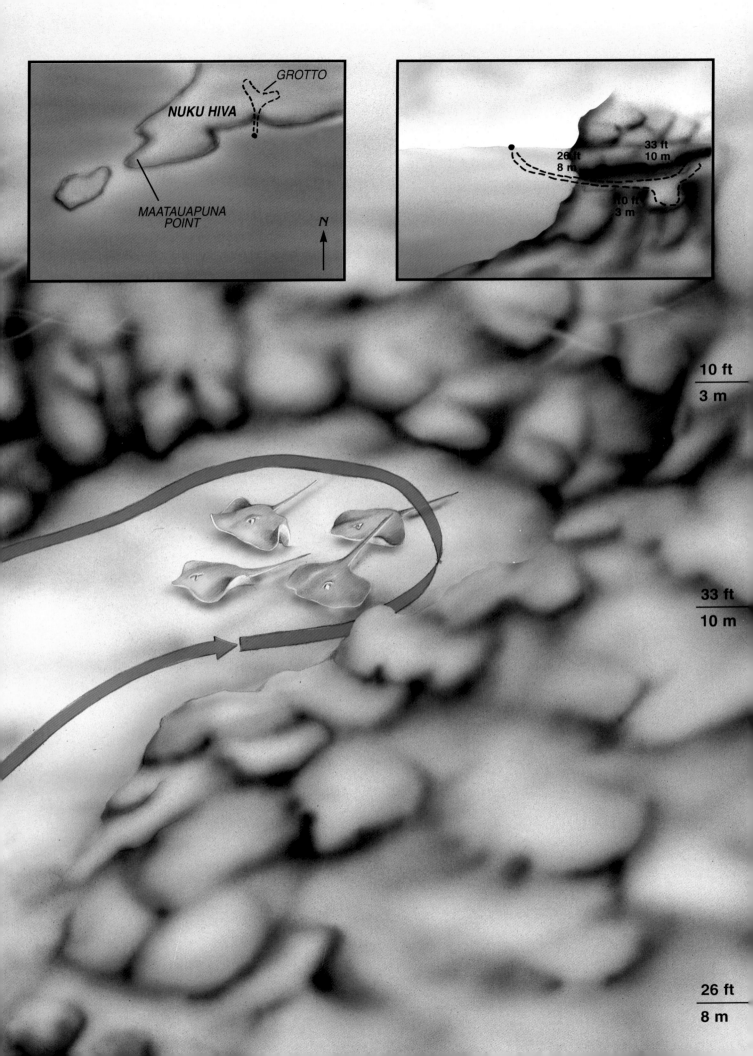

GROTTO

NUKU HIVA

MAATAUAPUNA
POINT

N

33 ft
10 m

26 ft
8 m

33 ft
10 m

10 ft
3 m

10 ft
3 m

33 ft
10 m

26 ft
8 m

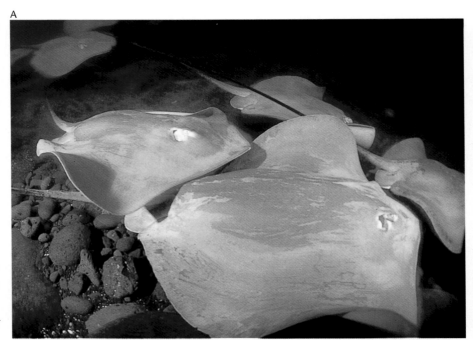
A

The site is located on the south side of Nuku Hiva island. From the dive center at the village of Taiohae, the boat follows the coast to Maatauapuna Point, to the east. The cave is not far from here, close to the steep rocky coast, but its entrance lies just under water and cannot be seen from the surface. At the bottom of the cave, the depth indicator shows about 26 feet (8 meters), sloping a little farther in to reach a final depth of 33 feet (10 meters).

Each diver must have a flashlight to explore the cave. Although it is possible to find the exit by following the walls even if the light breaks down, for safety

reasons it is a good idea to always carry a backup light. The cave is about 430 feet (131 meters) long. At its end, the tunnel narrows and leads farther into the island, but this part can only be explored with special equipment. As the map indicates, the cave is made up of two parts: a main corridor that leads directly north from the entrance, and a large area that opens to the east. The cave is quite spacious, and at no time will the divers have to swim through narrow passages.

So-called freshwater lenses, caused by rainwater filtering down through the roof of the cave to create a mixture of salt and fresh water called a halocline, produce strange optical illusions. In the last part of the main corridor, after a series of boulders populated by lobsters, there is a large airbell under the ceiling. It is possible to break through the surface here, but the regulator must not be removed, since the air may not contain sufficient oxygen. This site is suited to any diver with night diving experience, under the supervision of a dive guide.

The captain drops the divers off not far from the rocky shore. Depending on the swell, divers may have to swim against the waves until they reach the inside of the cave. Whitetip reef sharks often swim around the cave's entrance. Generally, the stingrays that give the site its name are concentrated in two points in the cave: at about 50 to 65 feet (15 to 20 meters) from the entrance where sunlight penetrates, and in the eastern section, in front of the back wall. It is advisable to switch on the flashlights and advance slowly. The stingrays live here in large schools of up to twenty-five members.

Stingrays eat all sorts of animals that they uncover in the sand, using their mouths, which are located under their bodies. They can reach a span of 5 feet (1.5 meters) and have a poisonous sting on the first third of heir tails. These stings are used only for defense, and are not a danger to swimmers or divers. Thanks to their sensitive sensory organs, stingrays are immediately alerted if someone enters the cave. With slow flapping movements, they rise from the sea bed and swim into the open sea or to another part of the cave.

Otherwise, small schools of soldier-fish and a few juvenile blacktip sharks swim close to the entrance.

C

D

E

B

A, C. The stingrays at Stingray Cave have set up house on the floor of the cave in two distinct areas: about 50 to 65 feet (15 to 20 meters) from the entrance, and in the back of the cave.

B. The 430-foot (130-meter)-long Stingray Cave does not require particular skill, but is still recommended only for experienced divers. Divers must also not forget to carry a flashlight to better admire the marvels in the cave.

D, F, G. The inside of Stingray Cave is not populated by fish other than the stingrays. However, a flashlight will reveal some extraordinary smaller creatures, such as shrimps (D), cicale di mare (F), and crabs (G, which also shows a paguro).

E. A large number of lobsters have made their den in the small holes and crevices of the reef near the main entrance to the cave.

F

G

MOTUMANO POINT

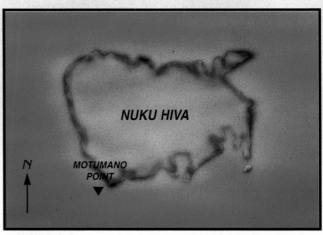

NUKU HIVA

MOTUMANO
POINT

N

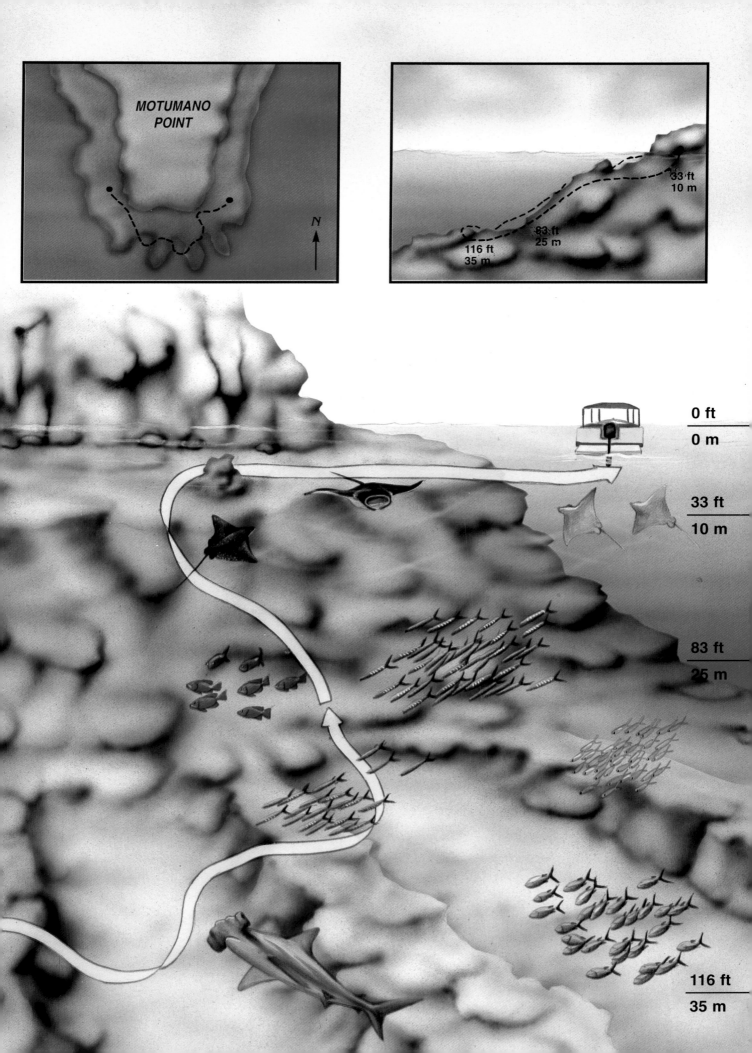

MOTUMANO POINT

N

0 ft
0 m

33 ft
10 m

83 ft
25 m

116 ft
35 m

33 ft
10 m

83 ft
25 m

116 ft
35 m

Motumano Point is a promontory that extends into the sea south of Nuku Hiva. Its position is already an indication that it hides an interesting underwater landscape. The coastal cliffs that rise high above the surface go to a depth of just 33 feet (10 meters), to form a flat strip that then goes in steps to a depth of 100 feet (30 meters), where it meets the sandy bed, on which several rock formations extend toward the open sea like huge fingers. In general, divers go into the water on the west side to swim underwater around the promontory, where they are picked up by the boat upon resurfacing. On the first platform, at 33 feet (10 meters) below the surface, one finds a large number of rock fragments that will be better examined toward the end of the dive. Following the classic dive profile, the deeper areas are visited first; ideally, you will have an underwater computer to precisely calculate nitrogen content. Once this platform is crossed, a drop extends for about 17 feet (5 meters), then another, and so on up to a depth of about 100 feet (30 meters), where the sandy seabed starts. Divers can stay close to this level until lack of time or air requires them to rise to shallower levels. Depending on the divers' skill and experience, the diving excursion may continue from this level toward the rock formations that go toward the open sea. In case of low visibility, it is very important to clearly remember the four cardinal points, so as not to lose your bearings. It is quite impossible to orient yourself without adequate instruments on a sandy surface. As a general rule, this dive, like most excursions around Nuku Hiva, must be undertaken with a dive guide.

After gradually rising over the

fissured rocky bottom, the divers come back to the strip of coastal rock, where they resurface, hearing rather than feeling the thundering of the waves as they break against the rocks. Only at the end of the dive should the divers swim a little in the open sea to reach the boat.

Single silvertip sharks swim in the open sea to the southeast, emerging briefly to disappear again after a few seconds. Hammerhead sharks patrol back and forth, and it is not unusual to

D

E

F

A. A solitary sea turtle prepares to leave the reef for the open ocean.

B. A fish tries to camouflage itself against the multicolored corals of Motumano.

C. The bright yellow mantle of a Murex gastropod stands out against the colors of the reef at Motumano Point.

D. The rich waters of Nuku Hiva, and in particular Motumano Point, are home to a wide variety of fish, such as this snapper.

the world of tiny creatures holds an unrivaled fascination. Sea urchins and starfish in these waters come in bizarre shapes and luminous colors.

Sea slugs can often be found among clumps of seaweed. Part of the mollusk family, these creatures, unlike snails, have no mobile home to which they can withdraw in case of danger. Instead, they defend themselves by means of a stinging poison that discourages predators. Snails—mollusks that carry their shells on their backs—can be found in the darker holes or on the ceilings of caves. The Marquesas Islands are a paradise for sea snails and sea slugs, and certain species such as the famous "Gauguini" are endemic to the area. The most beautiful are cowries, their highly polished oval shells often covered by a thick mantle.

It is much easier to observe mollusks while diving at night, when these nocturnal creatures leave their daytime hiding places to crawl over the sand and rocks in search of prey.

G

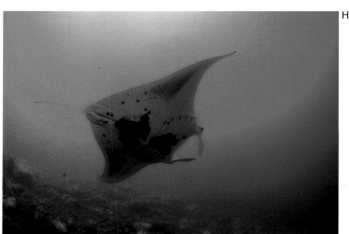

H

encounter the same shark several times. The same applies to manta rays, which are particularly abundant in the area. Jacks and barracudas can be found all over the place. But it is not only the great inhabitants of the deep that make diving at Motumano Point an interesting experience. It is well worthwhile to study just a single boulder to undertand the wealth of life concentrated in this microcosm of the reef. Many photographers swear that a glimpse of

E. A large stingray swims close to the bottom, foraging for food in waters rich in microorganisms.

F. Either disturbed by the photographer or on the hunt for prey, this large moray eel leaves its den.

G. The landscape of Nuku Hiva seems forbidding, with its bare vertical wall that drops off steeply into a sea abounding in life and color.

H. Looking out into the open sea, one can see manta rays that seem like ghosts or magical visions. These unusually shaped large creatures are very docile.

MATATEIKO POINT

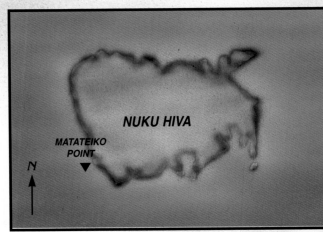

NUKU HIVA

MATATEIKO
POINT

N

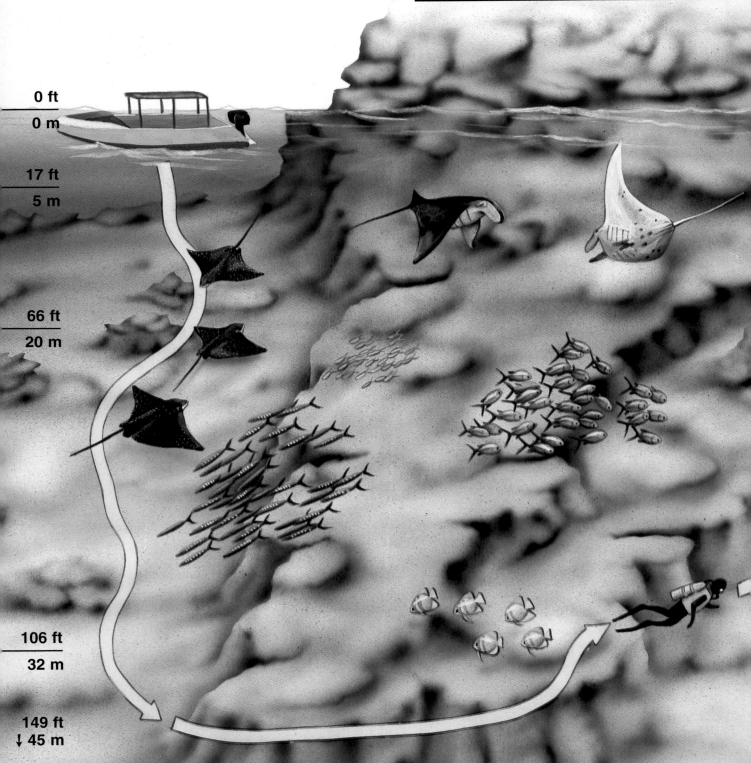

0 ft

0 m

17 ft

5 m

66 ft

20 m

106 ft

32 m

149 ft

45 m

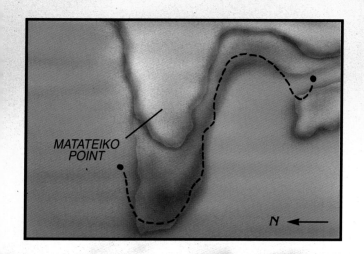

MATATEIKO POINT

N

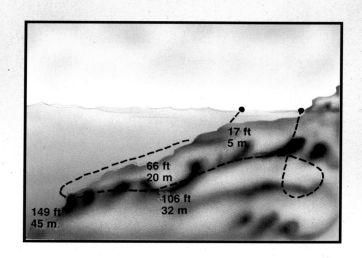

17 ft
5 m

66 ft
20 m

106 ft
32 m

149 ft
45 m.

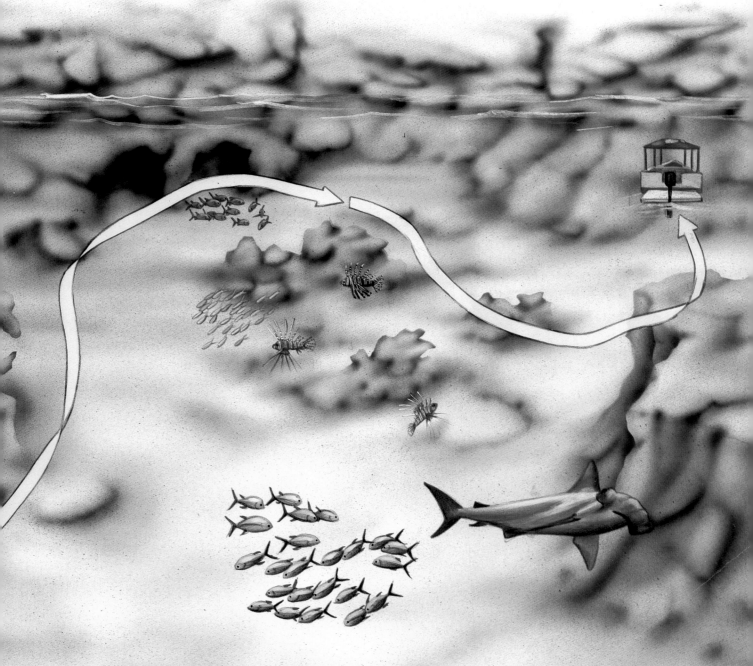

This dive site lies on the west side of Nuku Hiva, nearly at its southern end. Just where the steep cliffs of the island emerge from the sea, at a depth of about 17 feet (5 meters), an underwater rocky protuberance gradually slopes out to reach the sandy bottom at a depth of about 145 feet (44 meters). Large isolated rock formations lie on the bottom. At the southern end of the reef, again close to the steep rocky coast, at a depth of about 65 feet (20 meters), is a large cave with two entrances.

With a north or west wind, the sea is absolutely calm. With a south wind, a boat can drop off and pick up the divers in the protection of a small rocky bay.

The degree of difficulty of diving at Matateiko Point depends on the weather. With an absolutely calm sea, even divers with little experience can enjoy a dive, but if there is a current or waves, a higher level of skill is required. Generally, at this site the boat leaves the divers to the north of the rocky protuberance and picks them up to the south of it. Depending on the current and wind speed, the opposite procedure may be chosen, or dive parties may decide to resurface at the starting point. Immediately upon getting into the water, divers can follow the rockface. You must not lose sight of the bulge that opens into the sea. From here you can descend to the planned diving depth.

The area is full of high, sharp rock formations, interrupted by gorges. Divers who have never seen volcanic seabeds will be amazed at the underwater landscape. Visibility here in the Marquesas cannot be compared to that in the Tuamotu Islands, and therefore it is important to carefully observe the

A

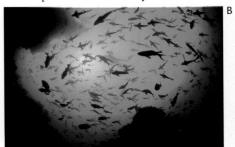
B

C

route described at the briefing and keep the correct distance from other divers, to maintain visibility. The sandy seabed starts at a depth of 145 (44 meters), and therefore it is not worthwhile to go deeper. Keeping the rocky edge to the right, divers should rise to a depth of about 65 feet (20 meters): once again, close to the rocky shore, the entrances to the cave come into view. It is well worthwhile to pay a short visit to the large cave with a flashlight. Sometimes you can find stingrays there, and there is a large school of soldierfish in front of the second exit. Depending on the diving plan, divers can continue along the rocky shore or return to the starting point, passing through shallow water above the rocky hump.

Even if underwater visibility in the Marquesas is not the best, the underwater landscape is unusual, rich in an unparalleled variety of fish. Scalloped hammerhead sharks are always patrolling around Matateiko Point. In the whole of Polynesia, one comes across this species only in the Marquesas. Matateiko Point is very similar to the Galapagos, with the same volcanic seabed, similar visibility, and deep waters in which the same sharks seem to come out of nowhere, only to

D

E

disappear again. The dive site, up to the point where the rocky bulge reaches the sandy seabed, is ideal for observing these sea creatures. As in the rest of the Marquesas, you seem to come across manta rays all over the place, swimming in circles in areas where the current brings them their staple diet, plankton. They are generally to be found immediately under the surface, but are not uncommon even at a depth of 100 feet (30 meters). Eagle rays prefer the north side of the rocky hump. They swim in the open sea, and therefore can be observed in the blue deep. One only finds two species of jacks in these waters: bigeye trevally (*Caranx sexfasciatus*) and giant trevally (*Caranx ignobilis*). The area around and between the rocks is literally teeming with life. Hundreds of individual unicornfish with their shining blue skin and all the classic Pacific reef-dwelling fish can be

found here. Under overhangs, in cracks and holes, one can find hundreds of lobsters, in close rows and sometimes even one on top of the other.

Well-camouflaged scorpionfish can be found in surprising numbers among the rocks. The sting of these fish is very painful. Stonefish, belonging to the same family, also have a poisonous sting, which can kill a man. Since they are well camouflaged, divers must be careful not to touch the reef or the seabed.

A. Pelagic species such as these silvertip reef sharks are common at Matateiko Point.

B. Sunlight penetrating through the blue waters reveals a multitude of fish.

C. The feared hammerhead sharks also frequent Matateiko Point.

D, E. Probably attracted by the plankton-rich waters at Matateiko Point, manta rays flit about close to the reef and in the open sea.

F. A solitary eagle ray rises from the open ocean.

G. This grouper, motionless over the reef, waits to ambush prey.

F

G

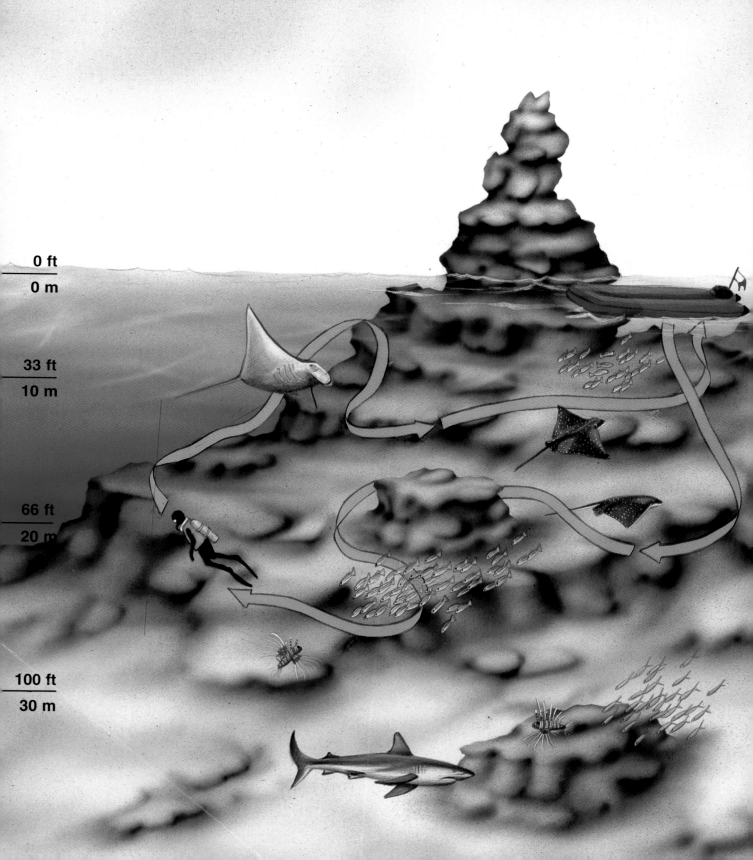

HATUATUA - INDIAN ROCK

0 ft
0 m

33 ft
10 m

66 ft
20 m

100 ft
30 m

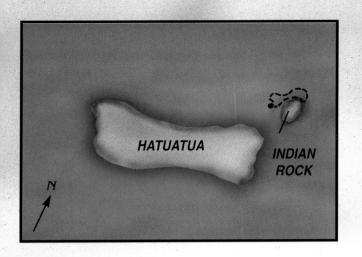

HATUATUA

INDIAN ROCK

N

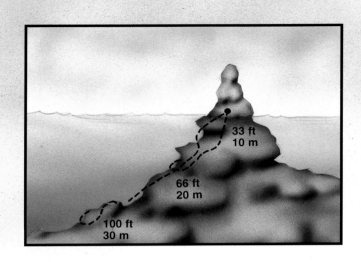

33 ft
10 m

66 ft
20 m

100 ft
30 m

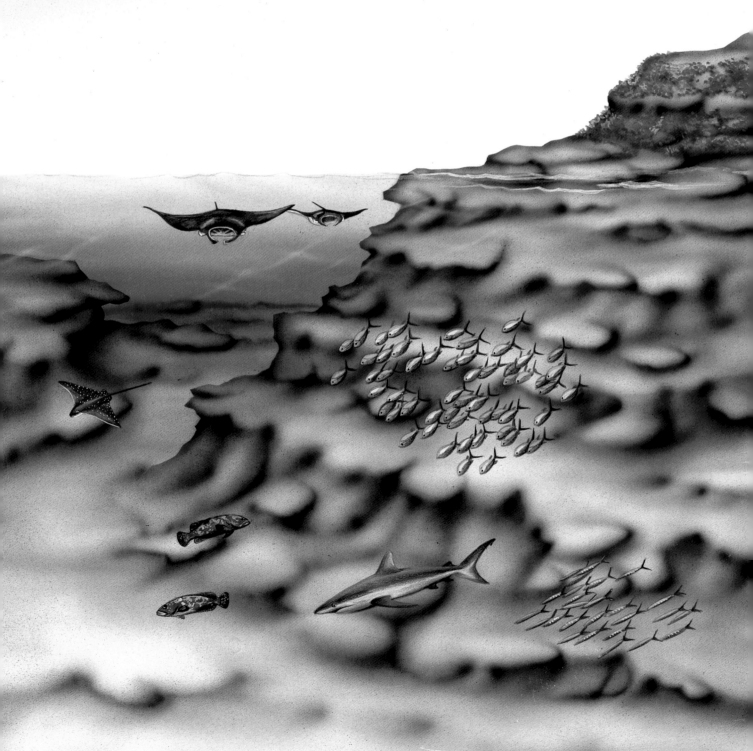

A

B

C

This dive site is located at the northwestern end of the small island of Hatuatua, also called Hatutu or Hatutaa on some maps. The northernmost island of the archipelago, it is located about 47 miles (75 kilometers) from Nuku Hiva. The impressive rock, which from a certain angle looks like an Indian squatting on the ground, can be seen from quite a distance. Just a narrow canal separates Indian Rock from the uninhabited island. With a north or east wind, the south side, leeward of the huge rocks, is well protected. It is advisable to start the dive from this point. Depending on the weather, boats drop divers off as close as possible to the rocks. The most interesting point is on the west, or northwest, side. To get there, you must follow the steep foot of the cliffs at a depth of 33 to 50 feet (10 to 15 meters). Since the seabed, which slopes at a 45-degree angle, is interrupted by large boulders, divers can choose a route that is always protected from the current, allowing for diving even with strong currents.

The slope ends at a depth of about 145 feet (44 meters), where rocks give

The huge numbers of groupers and scorpionfish are quite amazing.

These areas with strong currents are hunting grounds for mackerels, where large schools go after schools of sardines. It is impressive to see how the powerful steely bodies of the jacks shoot out to catch up with the prey and attack it at lightning speed. Gray reef sharks, silvertip sharks, and silky sharks are present everywhere. Because of the low visibility, one becomes aware of their presence only when they are very close. Divers should not be alarmed; with such an enormous amount of food available, the sharks don't seem at all interested in anything that does not look like a fish.

back when the pressure gauge indicates 1,000 psi. In bad weather, with wind and waves, bear in mind that you will have to swim quite a distance in the open sea before the boat picks you up.

The south side of the rock is also very interesting. The first few feet of the steep rock form an overhang that is splendidly covered. When there is no swell, this area is a paradise for macro-photographers.

The position of Indian Rock makes it a good spot for large fish. In the mostly calmer waters to the south, adult manta rays patrol to and fro. Mantas can be seen just under the surface or along the slope at a depth of 33 to 65 feet (10 to 20 meters). There is a well-established technique for touching manta rays. It is a mistake to swim toward them; you should swim in the same direction as the rays, and then remain completely still without moving. The ray will become aware of the diver's presence only at the last moment, sometimes at just arm's length, and will then veer sharply away.

The overhangs on the south side of the reef are wonderfully covered by corals. In the case of strong swells, divers must always maintain at least a 15-foot (5-meter) distance from the rock face, for safety reasons. The farther west you go, the richer the marine life.

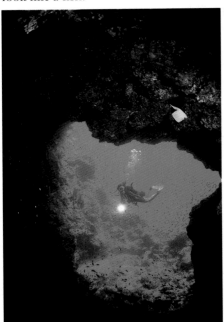

way to flat, sandy seabed. It is advisable to continue at a depth of 83 feet (25 meters), which gives you more bottom time. Much less air is needed for the return trip toward the south side of Indian Rock, since divers are swimming with the current. In any case, you must turn

A. The abundant marine life in the waters of Indian Rock attracts a large number of predators, such as these barracudas, which swim in shoals.

B. The large number of microorganisms in the waters at Indian Rock indicates that visibility is not as good as in other islands in French Polynesia.

C. A few melonhead sharks, having taken in their fill of air, return to the deep.

D. Indian Rock also features a large number of manta rays, easily distinguished by their individual belly coloring.

E. Indian Rock is a rock formation off the northwest tip of Hatuatua Island, 47 miles (75 kilometers) north of Nuku Hiva.

F. A diver approaches one of the caves in the wall at Indian Rock.

The Fish of French Polynesia

GINGLYMOSTOMATIDAE FAMILY

Tawny nurse shark
Nebrius ferrugineus

A shark with a cylindrical body; robust, flattened at the belly, with a broad, depressed snout. Subterminal mouth, with well-developed grooves at the nose and mouth; barbed nostrils. Teeth have a central cusp and a number of small cusps to the side. Dorsal fins at the rear, almost opposite the belly and anal fins; pectoral fins broad and scythe-shaped; caudal fin well developed, roughly one-third of the total length. Brownish gray and relatively dark in color. Feeds on fish, crustaceans, and cephalopods, which it inhales into its broad mouth. Ovoviviparous, measuring up to 11 feet (320 centimeters). Found from intertidal and shallow reefs to depths of 230 feet (70 meters) in the Indian and Pacific Oceans, from the Red Sea to Australia and as far as Tahiti.

RHINCODONTIAE FAMILY

Whale shark
Rhincodon typus

The largest living fish; can reach over 40 feet (12 meters) in length. Easily recognized by its bluish coloring and large white spots, and its body with longitudinal ribbing. The mouth is in a frontal position. Feeds exclusively on plankton and small fish. In spite of its size, this shark is harmless.

CARCHARHINIDAE FAMILY

Tiger shark
Galeocerdo cuvier

Without doubt one of the most dangerous of the sharks; it's a good idea to discover whether it is present in the waters. Recognized by its squat snout, nearly square head, and broad, dark stripes, which are less evident in larger examples. The teeth are subtriangular in shape, with rounded, serrated edges. During the day it tends to remain in deep water, coming to the surface during the night to hunt all manner of prey. Up to 22 feet (6.5 meters) long.

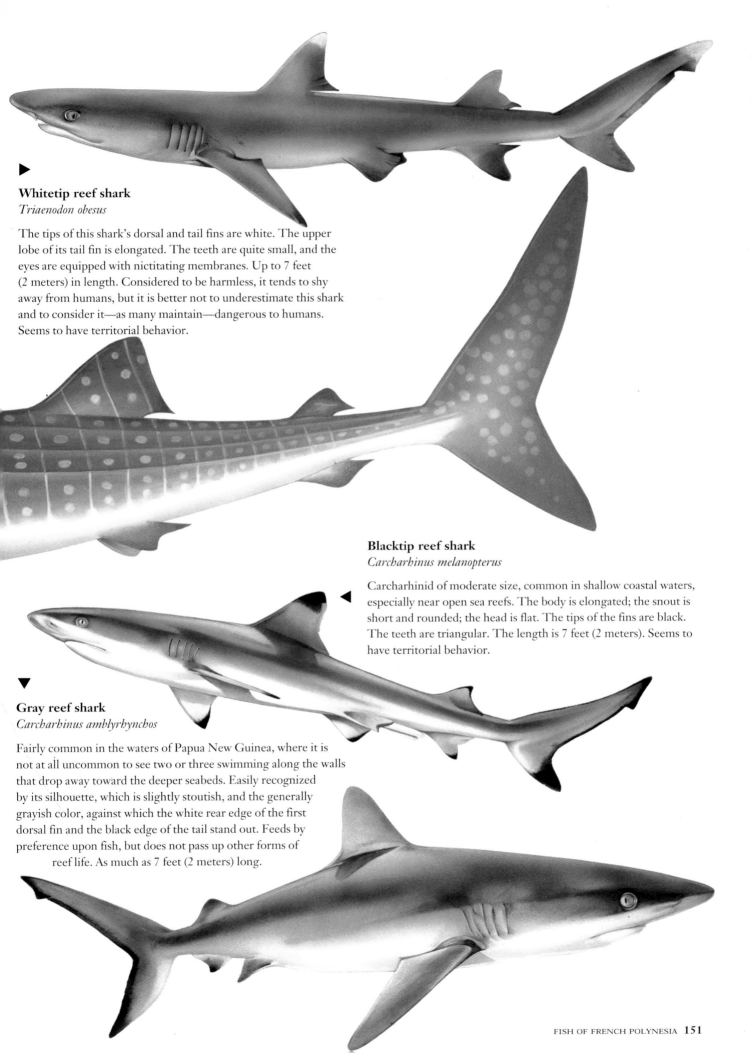

► **Whitetip reef shark**
Triaenodon obesus

The tips of this shark's dorsal and tail fins are white. The upper lobe of its tail fin is elongated. The teeth are quite small, and the eyes are equipped with nictitating membranes. Up to 7 feet (2 meters) in length. Considered to be harmless, it tends to shy away from humans, but it is better not to underestimate this shark and to consider it—as many maintain—dangerous to humans. Seems to have territorial behavior.

Blacktip reef shark
Carcharhinus melanopterus

Carcharhinid of moderate size, common in shallow coastal waters, especially near open sea reefs. The body is elongated; the snout is short and rounded; the head is flat. The tips of the fins are black. The teeth are triangular. The length is 7 feet (2 meters). Seems to have territorial behavior.

▼
Gray reef shark
Carcharhinus amblyrhynchos

Fairly common in the waters of Papua New Guinea, where it is not at all uncommon to see two or three swimming along the walls that drop away toward the deeper seabeds. Easily recognized by its silhouette, which is slightly stoutish, and the generally grayish color, against which the white rear edge of the first dorsal fin and the black edge of the tail stand out. Feeds by preference upon fish, but does not pass up other forms of reef life. As much as 7 feet (2 meters) long.

MOBULIDAE FAMILY

Manta ray
Manta birostris

▶

Easily recognized by its highly developed pectoral fins, which can reach a breadth of 16 to 20 feet (5 to 6 meters). The head has a pair of long, flat, and flexible cephalic fins, detached from the broad arch of the mouth. The upper jaw has no teeth. The long, thin tail has no bones. Dark back and white belly with black spots, whose arrangement makes it possible to distinguish one specimen from another.

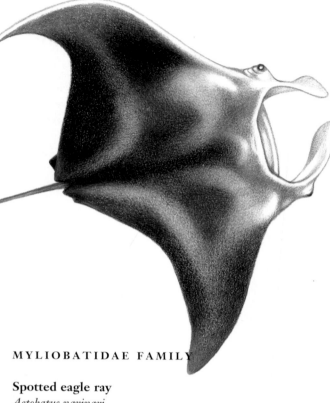

MYLIOBATIDAE FAMILY

◀

Spotted eagle ray
Aetobatus narinari

Easily recognized by its pointed, convex head, with large eyes and broad lateral spout holes. The lozenge-shaped body has broad, pointed pectoral fins. The tail, with one to five venomous spines, is around three times longer than the body. Broad, fleshy belly fins. The back is dark, with a large number of small white spots. Up to 8 feet (2.5 meters) wide. Can be found feeding in shallow lagoons with sandy beds from 3 to 17 feet (1 to 5 meters) deep.

DASYATIDAE FAMILY

Honeycomb stingray
Himantura uarnak

Disc-shaped body, broader than long. Pointed snout and very long tail. Prefers sandy seabeds among corals, or close to mangroves. Up to 6 feet (1.8 meters) in breadth. Common from the Red Sea to Polynesia.

▼

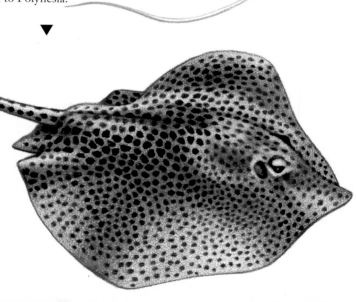

MURAENIDAE FAMILY

Giant moray
Gymnothorax javanicus

The largest of the morays, fairly common all across the Maldives. The body is powerful, rather tall on the trunk, and ends in a very well developed head. Short snout and wide mouth. The openings of the opercules are large and black and quite evident. Body marked by three rows of dark brown spots. The tail is reticulated. As long as 8 feet (2.5 meters).

Ribbon moray
Rhinomuraena quaesita

Ribbon-shaped eel, easily recognizable by its pointed snout and long jaws. Lower jaw has barbels; upper one has long, fringed nostrils. Young eels are blackish in color, males are blue with yellow fins, and females are all yellow. This species has a sexual inversion from male to female. Ribbon eels prefer sandy or detrital seabeds and generally leave only the front of their bodies exposed. Feeds on fish and crustaceans. Reaches 4 feet (1.2 meters) in length.

SYNODONTIDAE FAMILY

Variegated lizardfish
Synodus variegatus

Elongated body, compressed lengthwise. The head is convex toward the rear base. Eyes in an anterior-dorsal position. The snout is pointed, but short. The mouth is wide, and slightly oblique, the jaws well developed and equipped with numerous needle-shaped teeth. Variable coloring, but generally brownish on the back with more or less distinct red spots on the sides. Prefers sandy bottoms where it waits in ambush, poised on its sizable ventral fins.

HOLOCENTRIDAE FAMILY

Whitetipped soldierfish
Myripristis vittata

Sub-oval body with blunt snout and large eyes. Dorsal fin has sturdy, spiny, white-tipped rays that are the most distinctive feature of the species. Red-orange in color. Lives in groups in grottoes and less illuminated areas of the reef. Up to 8 inches (20 centimeters) in size.

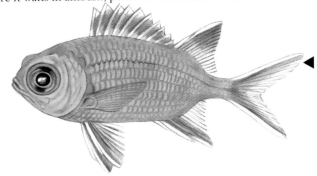

Saber squirrelfish
Sargocentron spiniferum

Wide, fairly compressed body. Pointed snout with relatively large eyes. Dorsal fin is well developed, with a red interradial membrane. Body is red with red spots, which are darker on the operculum and at the base of the pectoral fins. A nocturnal species, it has an aggressive nature due to its territorial habits. Up to 18 inches (45 centimeters) long.

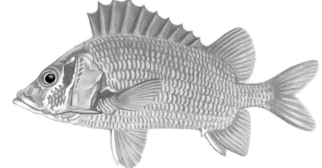

Crown squirrelfish
Sargocentron diadema

This squirrelfish has an oval body, longer and not so high as that of the saber squirrelfish. It has large eyes, as it too has nocturnal habits. Red in color, with white stripes on the sides. A white band runs along the bottom of its snout to the opercules; the front of the dorsal fin is black. Measures 10 inches (25 centimeters).

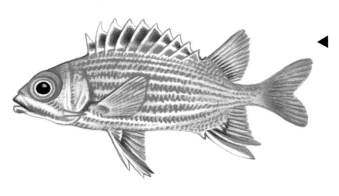

ANOMALOPIDAE FAMILY

Flashlightfish
Anomalops katoptron

Rounded in shape, with two dorsal fins and a decidedly forked, almost black tail. The main distinguishing feature of this nocturnal fish is the large light-emitting organ below the eye, which can be switched on and off by means of an opaque membrane. Lives in grottoes and clefts in the reef. Up to 5 inches (12 centimeters) in length.

AULOSTOMIDAE FAMILY

Chinese trumpetfish
Aulostomus chinensis

Elongated, compressed body ending in a long tubular snout with a small mouth, barbed beneath the jaw. A number of erect spines are found at the center of the back. The second dorsal fin is close to the caudal peduncle, opposite the anal fin. Color varies from gray to greenish. Feeds on small fish and crustaceans. Reaches a length of 24 inches (60 centimeters).

FISTULARIIDAE FAMILY

Bluespotted cornetfish
Fistularia commersonii

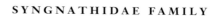

Cylindrical body ends in a long, tubular snout. Dorsal and anal fins are symmetrical and situated well to the rear. Caudal fin has two very thin and elongated central wings. Coloring varies due to the exceptional ability of this fish to camouflage itself, remaining in ambush to capture the small prey it feeds on. Can often be seen swimming hidden by the bodies of larger, harmless fish, to approach its prey unseen. Up to 5 feet (1.5 meters) in length.

SYNGNATHIDAE FAMILY

Schultz's pipefish
Corythoichthys schultzi

Not an easy fish to spot, due its ability to camouflage itself and its small size. Thin body and long snout; well-developed eyes. Profile of the back appears slightly toothed due to the special shape of the stiff rings that form the body. The caudal fin is reddish, with white edges. There are 5 rows on orange points along the body. Lives in the flat zones of the reef and feeds on tiny crustaceans. Reaches a length of 6.5 inches (16 centimeters).

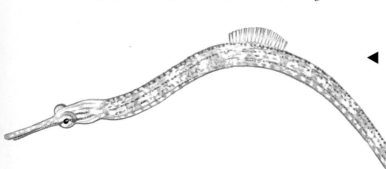

Spotted seahorse
Hippocampus kuda

A seahorse with the unmistakable shape. The bony plates that cover the body have small protuberances. Coloring varies, and is often similar to that of the surrounding environment. Lives along the coastal reefs and in brackish water, up to a depth of 100 feet (30 meters). Measures up to 12 inches (30 centimeters).

SYNANCEIIDAE FAMILY

Stonefish
Synanceia verrucosa

This fish has a moderate oblong body, compressed at the sides and free of scales. The head is massive, covered with crests and spines, and the eyes are turned up, as is the wide mouth. The pectoral fins are very well developed. Coloring provides excellent camouflage, and the fish is virtually identical to a stone. The glands at the base of the spines produce a powerful poison, which can be fatal. It attains 14 inches (35 centimeters) in length.

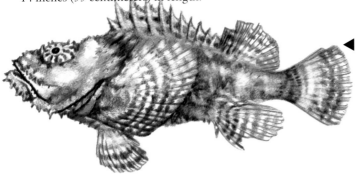

Turkeyfish (lionfish)
Pterois volitans

Body similar to the previous species. Coloring presents broad brown vertical stripes; not all the same width. The rays of the fins are not naked, but possess a more or less developed membrane reminiscent of feathers. The odd-numbered fins bear rows of brownish black spots. Around the mouth and above the eyes are some indented appendages.

SCORPAENIDAE FAMILY

False stonefish (devil scorpionfish)
Scorpaenopsis diabolus

A slightly oval body, massive and high, with numerous fleshy excrescences. The large head is covered with spines; the mouth is wide and turns up. The pectoral fins extend to the anal fin. Coloring provides excellent camouflage, as this species hunts from ambush. Tail fin has broad, dark vertical stripes. The spines of the dorsal fin are poisonous, but not to the same degree as those of the stonefish. Grows to a length of 12 inches (30 centimeters).

Clearfin turkeyfish (radial firefish)
Pterois radiata

Oblong body with a large head and a large mouth. The rays of the pectoral fins, which are very long, do not branch out, and the upper ones are joined by a membrane, but only at the base. All of the rays are poisonous. The body is a brownish red with white stripes. Above the eyes are long, fleshy papillae. Can attain a size of 10 inches (25 centimeters).

Leaf scorpionfish
Taenianotus triacanthus

Typical scorpionfish shape; large head, oblique mouth, and compression and tapering toward the rear. Fragmented appendices above the eye. Dorsal fin very large; venomous spinous rays. Variable and mimetic coloring allows the fish to advance slowly, like a leaf borne on the current, upon the smaller fish upon which it feeds. Up to 4 to 5 inches (10 to 12 centimeters) long.

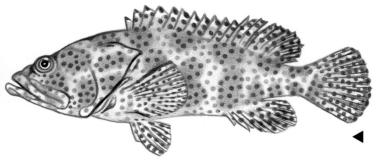

Camouflage grouper
Epinephelus polyphekadion

Distinctive coloring, with the pale upper part of the body showing dark streaks. Prefers the richer areas of the coral, where it captures mainly crustaceans. Measures up to 30 inches (75 centimeters). Common from the Red Sea to Australia.

Blacktip grouper
Epinephelus fasciatus

Tapering body, with a rather low dorsal fin. Generally pale in color, with more or less marked reddish brown vertical stripes. Head bears a broad reddish spot, and the tips of the spines on the dorsal fin are black. Prefers the outer slopes of the reef and can often be seen resting on coral. Measures up to 16 inches (40 centimeters) in length.

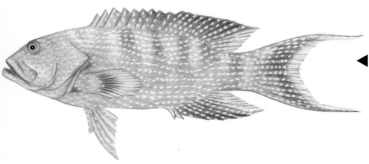

GRAMMISTIDAE FAMILY

Sixline soapfish
Grammistes sexlineatus

High, compressed, oval body, covered with very small scales. Broad mouth; small fleshy growth on the lower jaw. Easily recognized by yellowish white horizontal stripes reaching from the head to the peduncle, which stand out strongly against the dark brown, bluish body. When frightened it emits a mucus poisonous to other fish.

SERRANIDAE FAMILY

Peacock hind
Cephalopholis argus

Massive body, spindle-shaped, slightly compressed. Robust head, with a slightly protruding lower jaw. Edge of the caudal fin rounded. Dorsal fin has nine spiny rays and a rounded rear edge, which ends at the height of the caudal peduncle, like the anal fin. Has a number of blue spots and ten dark stripes on the sides. Dark blue fins. Reaches 20 inches (50 centimeters) in length.

Greasy grouper
Epinephelus tauvina

Tapered body, slightly compressed, and lower than that of the other groupers. Pointed snout, with a broad mouth. Caudal fin is rounded, and the rather low dorsal fin has spiny rays. Along the back, at the base of the dorsal fin, are a number of large dark spots. Smaller spots are distributed throughout the body, whose base color is pale. This species can grow to over 6.5 feet (2 meters) in length.

Yellow-edged lyretail
Variola louti

Spindle-shaped body, ending in a broad caudal peduncle that supports an unmistakable scythe-shaped tail, with elongated lobes. The dorsal and anal fins have a pointed rear edge. Reddish or brownish, with hints of purple and a number of paler spots. A widespread species; 32 to 34 inches (80 to 85 centimeters) in length.

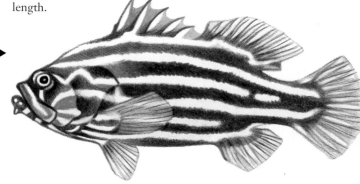

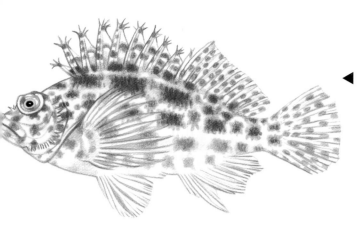

PRIACANTHIDAE FAMILY

Crescent tail bigeye
Priacanthus hamrur

Oval, tall, compressed body. Short snout, and large eyes that stand out, revealing nocturnal habits. Mouth turned upward. Caudal fin shaped like a crescent moon, with elongated lobes, especially in adults. Generally a dark reddish hue, but can change rapidly, acquiring more or less pronounced silvery highlights or becoming striped with red on silvery body. Dorsal and anal fins have dark highlights along their edges. Attains a length of 16 to 18 inches (40 to 45 centimeters).

CARANGIDAE FAMILY

Bluefin trevally
Caranx melampygus

Elongated, rather tall body; terminates in a convex head and a high forehead. Small eyes. Caudal peduncle is narrow and reinforced with visible bony plates; lateral line is complete and arched anteriorly. Greenish brown, with numerous small black spots. Long, sickle-shaped pectoral fins with scales on their sides, yellow in the young of the species. Grows to be longer than 3 feet (1 meter).

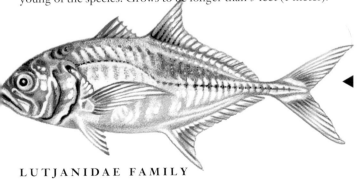

LUTJANIDAE FAMILY

Bluestriped snapper
Lutjanus kasmira

Tapered body; pointed snout. Large eyes and mouth. Dorsal fin extends to the height of the caudal peduncle. Golden yellow back, paler sides, and almost silvery belly. Four light lengthwise stripes, the longest running from mouth to caudal peduncle. Dorsal and caudal fins edged in black. Measures 16 inches (40 centimeters) in length.

CIRRHITIDAE FAMILY

Pixy hawkfish
Cirrhitichthys oxycephalus

Massive, tall body, compressed toward the front. Dorsal profile appears concave in line with the eyes, which protrude slightly to allow the fish to observe its surroundings while resting on the bottom. Dorsal fin has fringing at the tip of the spinous rays. Whitish, with dark brown spots edged with red; fins are spangled with red. Feeds chiefly on small crustaceans, and grows to a length of 3 inches (7 centimeters).

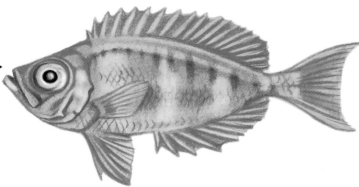

ECHENEIDAE FAMILY

Sharksucker
Echeneis naucrates

Elongated body, flattened at the back. Typically associated with larger fish such as sharks and mantas, to which it adheres using the sucker created from the dorsal fin. Feeds on the parasites of the fish to which it attaches itself, but can swim and hunt independently. Up to 3.5 feet (1.1 meters) in length.

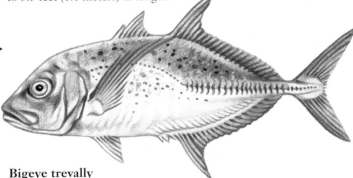

Bigeye trevally
Caranx sexfasciatus

Elongated and compressed body; rounded forward silhouette. Lower jaw tends to jut. Evident keels on the caudal stalk; caudal fin sharply forked. Blue-gray or blue-green back; lobes of the caudal fin show a blackish hue. Greenish yellow or silvery sides. The young of the species are golden yellow, with four to seven broad dark vertical bands. Grows to be longer than 4.5 feet (1.5 meters).

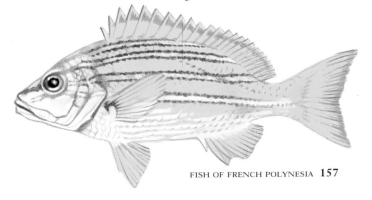

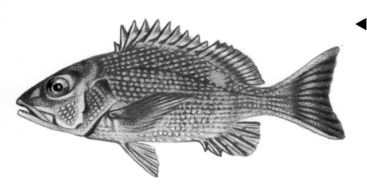

Two-spot red snapper
Lutjanus bohar

Massive body, rather tall and rounded. Large eyes and a wide mouth with sharp pointed teeth. Sight incision in the area in front of the gills. Caudal fin broad, slightly indented; pectoral fins scythe-shaped and well developed. Reddish bronze back, paler belly. Two pronounced mother-of-pearl spots at the base of the dorsal fin. Lives in the deeper parts of the barrier reef. Up to 20 inches (50 centimeters) long.

Humpback red snapper
Lutjanus gibbus

Massive, tall, compressed body. Pointed snout, but the larger examples have a dorsal profile that is concave at the height of the eyes. Deep incision in front of the gills. Caudal fin clearly indented, with rounded lobes. Brownish green back, becoming reddish on the sides and belly, with meshlike scales. Yellow eyes, lips, and base of pectorals. Lives in schools in relatively deep waters along the reef. Up to 16 inches (40 centimeters) long.

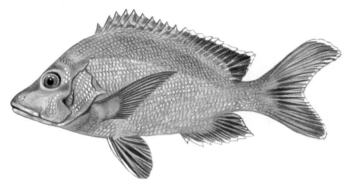

MULLIDAE FAMILY

Yellowfin goatfish
Mulloidichthys vanicolensis

Elongated body, nearly flat in the belly, and taller in the frontal parts. Small mouth; barbs typical of the family beneath the chin. Distinctive coloring, with a yellow stripe running from the eye to the tail; yellow fins. During the day, this species lives in dense shoals that gather close to sandy seabeds. An active hunter by night. Up to 15 inches (38 centimeters) in length.

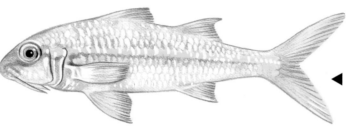

Goldsaddle goatfish
Parupeneus cyclostomus

Tall, tapering body ending in a protruding snout. Lower jaw has two long barbs that reach the ventral fins. Two dorsal fins, distinctly separate from each other. Tail has twin lobes. The head bears more or less marked bluish streaks, and the second dorsal fin has a dark spot at the rear. Younger examples are more brightly colored. Measures 14 inches (35 centimeters) in length.

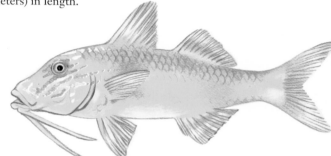

EPHIPPIDAE FAMILY

Orbicular batfish
Platax orbicularis

Rounded body, mainly due to the size of the dorsal and anal fins. Pale, with dark vertical stripes. Anal and dorsal fins edged in black. Lives close to the reef, above the sandy seabed, and feeds on benthic invertebrates and plankton. Measures up to 20 inches (50 centimeters) in length.

CHAETODONTIDAE FAMILY

Raccoon butterflyfish
Chaetodon lunula

Oval body ends in a pointed snout; a broad black and white stripe conceals the eyes. Golden yellow sides; thin stripes form a broad dark spot on the back. A diagonal black band runs from the head to the back. Nocturnal in its habits but relatively active during the day, gathering in shoals. Up to 8.5 inches (21 centimeters) long.

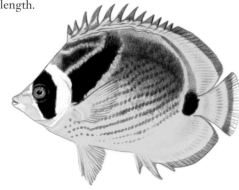

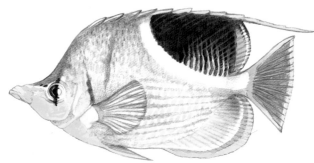

Threadfin butterflyfish
Chaetodon auriga

Nearly rectangular body, very tall and compressed. Head is concave toward the front, and terminates in a pointed, short snout. A broad dark band covers the eye, narrowing on the back. Dorsal fin features a dark ocellate spot along the rearmost edge, topped by a number of elongated and filamentous rays that constitute one of the distinctive features of this species. Swims alone or in pairs. Measures 8 to 10 inches (20 to 25 centimeters) in length.

Longnose butterflyfish
Forcipiger longirostris

Extremely distinctive in shape, easy to recognize by the long beak-like snout and the truncated rear portion of the body. Upper section of the head is black, while the lower section is lighter in color, with silvery highlights. Yellow body, with a few dark stripes at the base of the pectoral fin. Transparent caudal fin. Lives in small groups of five to six individuals, and feeds on small invertebrates that it captures in the nooks and crannies of the coral with its long snout. Up to 8 inches (20 centimeters) in length.

Masked bannerfish
Heniochus monocero

Tall, slightly oval, compressed body; massive head; distinctively concave from base of dorsal fin to eye. Short, pointed snout. Rear edges of dorsal and anal fin rounded. Fourth ray of the dorsal fin very long and well developed, especially in adult males. Truncated caudal fin. Coloration characterized by three dark bands separated by white areas; yellow dorsal and caudal fins. Live in pairs or in small groups along outer reef. Up to 10 inches (25 centimeters) long.

Saddle butterflyfish
Chaetodon ephippium

High, compressed body; dorsal fin elongated toward the rear. Large black spot with a red-orange border extends on the rear portion of the body between the dorsal fin and tail stump. Lives in lagoons and on the outer reef at 100 to 132 feet (30 to 40 meters) below the surface. Feeds mainly, but not exclusively, on coral polyps; diet also includes invertebrates, sponges, seaweed, and fish eggs. Sometimes found in shoals. Up to 9 inches (23 centimeters) in length.

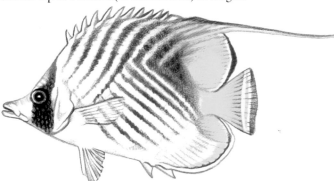

Melon butterflyfish
Chaetodon trifasciatus

Compressed oval body; pointed snout with a small mouth at its tip. Body is whitish yellow, with fine purple stripes on the flanks; eyes are covered by a black band. Territorial; lives in pairs in protected coral-rich areas up to 65 feet (20 meters) below the surface. It grows to a length of up to 6 inches (15 centimeters).

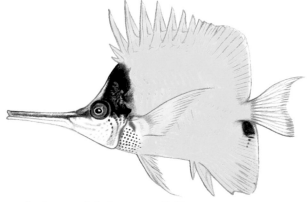

Longfin bannerfish (pennant fish)
Heniochus acuminatus

High, compressed body terminating in a short snout. Basic coloring is whitish with two black bands; the first stretches from the dorsal fin to the ventral fins, and the second covers part of the anal fin. Eyes disguised by a black band; yellow tail fin. Dorsal fin terminates in a distinctive long filament.
Prefers to live in pairs.
Up to 10 inches
(25 centimeters).

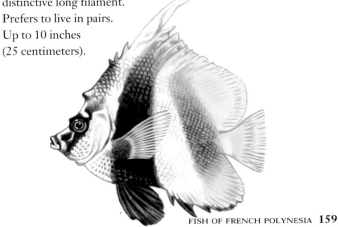

Lemonpeel angelfish
Centropyge flavissimus

Compressed, oval body. Small mouth, with tiny teeth resembling pincers. Lives in haremlike groups made up of one male and a number of females. Prefers the rich zones of the coral lagoons and outer reefs, to a depth of 85 feet (26 meters). Feeds on algae. Measures up to 6 inches (15 centimeters) in length.

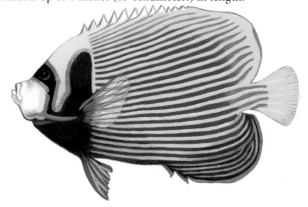

POMACENTRIDAE FAMILY

Indo-Pacific Sergeant
Abdudefduf vaigiensis

Oval body; convex snout, small mouth with conical incisor teeth. Commonly found in a wide variety of habitats, including lagoons, flat seabeds, and reef slopes. Lives in shoals and feeds on zooplankton, small invertebrates, and algae on the seabed. Up to 8 inches (20 centimeters) in length.

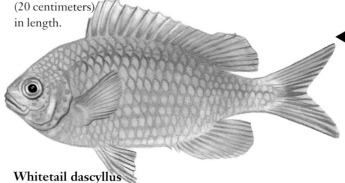

Whitetail dascyllus
Dascyllus aruanus

Relatively squat, square, tall, and compressed body; mouth is small, with a slightly protruding lower jaw. Base coloring is whitish with three clear transverse dark bands, the first of which covers the eye and mouth. Forms small groups, each closely linked to a single madrepore colony. Only the larger individuals move away from the coral, while the smaller ones remain among the madrepore branches. Measures 3 to 4 inches (8 to 10 centimeters) in length.

POMACANTHIDAE FAMILY

Royal angelfish
Pygoplites diacanthus

Less tall than other angelfish. Rear edges of the dorsal and caudal fins well developed, but do not extend beyond the caudal area. Yellowish orange, with eight to nine blue stripes. The eyes are surrounded by two distinct blue streaks. Dorsal fin has more or less dark streaks; anal fin has yellow stripes parallel to the fin surrounds. Immature specimens have a spot behind the eye. Measures 10 to 12 inches (25 to 30 centimeters) in length.

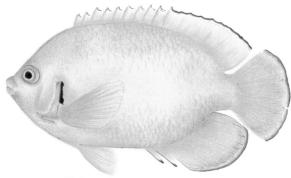

Emperor angelfish
Pomacanthus imperator

Body tends towards an oval shape; tall and compressed, with a short snout, protractile mouth, and thick lips. Eyes are surrounded by a black spot edged in blue; sides striped blue and yellow. Front of the snout is dark blue in the males and pale blue in the females. The young fish have a blue-and-white concentric stripe design. Territorial in habits; lives close to grottoes and sheltered rocks. Measures up to 15 inches (38 centimeters) in length.

Blue-green damselfish
Chromis viridis

Virtually identical in shape to the damselfish of the Mediterranean. Bluish green in varying intensity, with slight hints of gold along the edges of the scales. A gregarious fish that tends to gather in large groups, each of which seems to colonize a clearly determined madreporic formation, preferring those found close to the vertical walls in the outer part of the reef. Measures 3 to 4 inches (8 to 10 centimeters) in length.

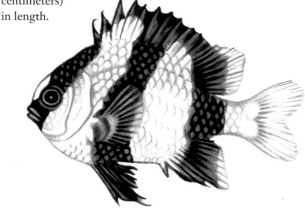

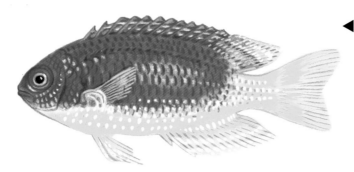

LABRIDAE FAMILY

Slingjaw wrasse
Epibulus insidiator

Wide, robust body. Large head and mouth characterized by protruding jaws, capable of forming a sort of large tube when completely extended. Females are totally yellow. Males have a white head. In both sexes a black streak crosses the eyes. An active predator, it feeds on fish and crustaceans. Up to 14 inches (35 centimeters) long.

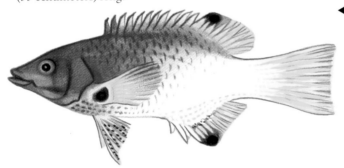

Napoleon wrasse (humphead wrasse)
Cheilinus undulatus

The largest known member of the Labridae family; has a very distinctive tall and stubby structure. The mouth is large and features thick protractile lips that allow this fish literally to suck up its prey. In adults, the head is marked by a pronounced bump on the forehead. Greenish gray, with irregular greenish yellow stripes along the sides, shifting to orange on the head. These fish can be as long as 7 feet (2.1 meters), and can weigh up to 400 pounds (180 kilograms).

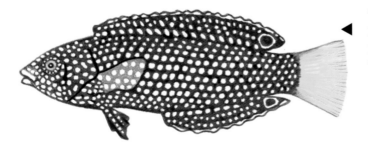

Clown wrasse
Coris gaimard

Tapered, slender body. The first two rays of the dorsal fin are typically elongated in adult males. The color is dusty, with blue spots on the back and pale forehead. The head is tapered with green bands. The caudal fin is yellow. Juveniles are red with black-edged white saddles. Up to 14 to 16 inches (35 to 40 centimeters) long.

Caerulean damselfish
Pomacentrus caeruleus

Lives solitary or in shoals along the outer slope of reefs, close to large masses of corals or detritus. It measures up to 4 inches (10 centimeters) and is found from eastern Africa to the Maldives.

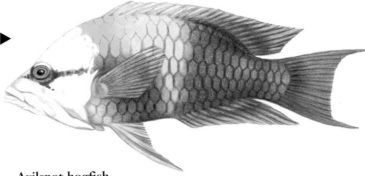

Axilspot hogfish
Bodianus axillaris

Tapered and compressed body; pointed snout. The ventral fins are well developed, and the longer ventral rays reach almost to the anal aperture. Caudal fin is truncated in adults and rounded in the young. The forward portion of the body is dark and contrasts sharply with the lighter hue of the rest. The base of the pectoral, dorsal, and anal fins have a pronounced dark spot. The young specimens have nine white spots on their bodies. Up to 8 inches (20 centimeters) long.

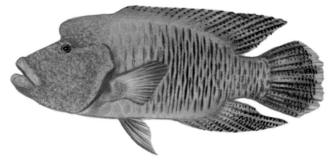

Yellowtail wrasse (spotted wrasse)
Anampses meleagrides

Tapered body with a generally oval silhouette and a slight frontal hump, more pronounced in females. The mouth is terminal, and protractile, with large fleshy lips. Adult males are dark and purplish, with more-or-less-elongated bluish spots along the edge of the scales. Dorsal and anal fins feature bluish stripes, as does the rearmost edge of the caudal fin, the lobes of which are elongated. Females are dark, spangled with numerous white spots. Snout and lower head are reddish. Caudal fin is yellow. Up to 10 inches (25 centimeters) in length.

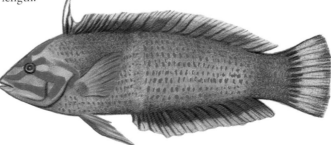

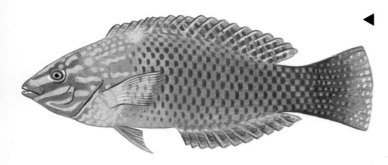

Checkerboard wrasse
Halichoeres hortuanus

Elongated, compressed body; well-developed head and pointed snout, with the mouth at the end. Changes sex from female to male. Males have a green head with orange and pink stripes and spots up to the height of the pectoral fins. The body is blue-green with dark spots at the center of the scales, which resemble squares on a chess board. Tail is edged in red. The female has a yellow tail; rear part of the body is reddish, with a black spot on the back. Grows to 10 inches (25 centimeters) in length.

Bluestreak cleaner wrasse
Labroides dimidiatus

Compressed body, elongated and covered in large scales. Head is pointed. The snout is elongated, with a small mouth at the end, bearing a large number of tiny pointed teeth. Upper jaw is longer. The brownish front half of the body is darker on the back than on the belly. A broad black stripe runs from the start of the snout to the end of the caudal fin, widening as it goes. The base of the anal fin and the rear part of the body are intense blue in color. Reaches 4 inches (10 centimeters) in length.

SCARIDAE FAMILY

Blue-barred parrotfish
Scarus ghobban

Oval body, tall and slightly compressed. Rounded snout, with thick lips that reveal the white teeth at certain points. Short, robust caudal peduncle. Caudal fin is slightly crescent-shaped, with pointed lobes. The female is generally reddish yellow, with vertical blue bands. The male has no blue bands, but there are blue streaks on the lips and from the mouth to the eye. The scales on the body are edged in blue; the odd fins are shot through with red. Up to 24 inches (60 centimeters) long.

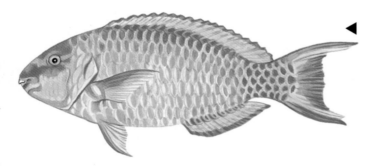

Daisy parrotfish
Scarus sordidus

General shape of the body is typical of the parrotfish. The dental plates are clearly visible. The young fish have horizontal stripes. As they grow, they turn green, with the edges of the scales salmon pink. Cheeks are bright orange, shading into yellow around the gills. Strangely, the teeth are green, while the females have a red mouth. Up to 16 to 20 inches (40 to 50 centimeters) long.

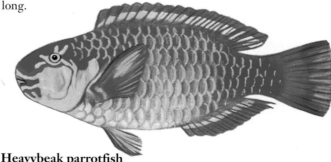

Heavybeak parrotfish
Scarus gibbus

Oval body, tall and robust. Front profile of the head highly convex, almost vertical. The dental plates are not clearly visible. Three rows of large scales on the cheeks. Caudal fin is a half-moon shape. Brownish yellow body; the lower part of the snout is green in the females, with pink stripes of varying intensity on the scales. These can also be found in the males, which have a greenish back shading to violet. The belly is bluish green. The rear edge of the caudal fin is green. Reaches a length of 28 inches (70 centimeters).

♀

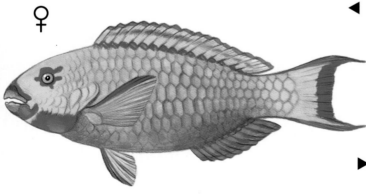

♂

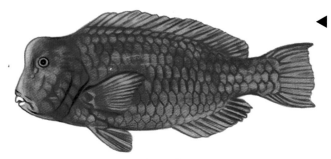

SPHYRAENIDAE FAMILY

Great barracuda ▶
Sphyraena barracuda

Elongated, slightly cylindrical body. Snout is long and pointed, and lower jaw is prominent. Teeth are numerous and canine-shaped. There are two dorsal fins, clearly separated. The coloring ranges from grayish to greenish brown on the back, while the sides and the belly are silvery. The adults have irregular dark spots along their sides near the caudal fin. Attains a length of 6 feet (1.8 meters).

BLENNIIDAE FAMILY

Leopard blenny
Exallias brevis

A large blenny, with a massive body and rather high dorsal fin. Typically features widespread red spotting on the body but not on the head. Females are less colorful than males. The species generally lives among colonies of branched madrepores and fire coral. It feeds on coral polyps. Males are territorial and at the time of reproduction, prepare a nest in the coral to which they attract females to lay their eggs. Grows up to about 6 inches (15 centimeters) in length.

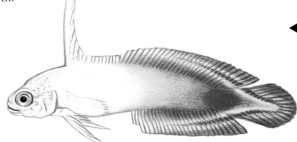

ZANCLIDAE FAMILY

Moorish idol ▶
Zanclus cornutus

Tall, compressed, disk-shaped body. The dorsal profile of the head is rounded, but inclined. Tubular snout, with a terminal mouth endowed with long teeth resembling bristles. The third ray of the dorsal fin constitutes the most distinctive feature of the species. These fish form small schools and are omnivorous. Up to 10 inches (25 centimeters) in length.

◀ ### Bumphead parrotfish
Bolbometopon muricatum

Wide, compressed body, unmistakable due to the clearly visible protuberance on the back of the head and an almost vertical front profile. Mouth partially turned downward. Generally a brownish color, and young individuals are characterized by five vertical lines of small white dots on their flanks. Lives in groups to a depth of 100 feet (30 meters), and feeds on corals and encrusted algae. Up to 4 feet (1.2 meters) long.

Blackfin barracuda
Sphyraena qenie

Elongated body, typical of the barracuda. The lower jaw, devoid of any fleshy excrescence, is prominent, but the back of the jaw goes no farther back than the forward margin of the eye. First dorsal fin begins after the pectoral fins; second dorsal fin is symmetrical with the anal fin. Caudal fin is forked, and strangely can have three lobes in the larger specimens. Silvery, with eighteen to twenty-two dark vertical bands. The dorsal and caudal fins are dark, as is the anal fin, while the last two anal rays are white. Up to 4 feet (1.2 meters) long.

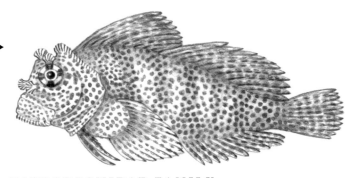

MICRODESMIDAE FAMILY

Fire goby
Nemateleotris magnifica

Elongated body, rounded toward the front and compressed to the rear. Short snout, large eyes. Wide mouth, with many teeth, including large canines. Two dorsal fins; broad, rounded caudal fin; separate ventral fins. Light coloration, with yellow highlights at the front; red with black-striped fins at the rear. Territorial; lives in dens dug into the sand, where it hides when threatened. Up to 3 inches (7 centimeters) long.

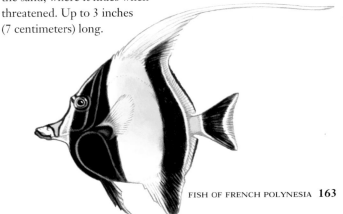

Sailfin tang
Zebrasoma veliferum

Compressed, tall, rounded body due to the significant development of the fins. The profile of the head is concave. Short snout, with a protracting mouth at the end. Adults are brownish, with alternating pale and dark stripes that continue into the dorsal fin and anal fins, together with thin orange streaks. Live in couples or in small shoals. Up to 16 inches (40 centimeters) in length.

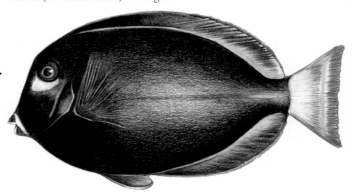

Black surgeonfish
Acanthurus gahhm

Oval body, tall and slightly compressed. Rounded frontal profile. The dorsal and anal fins are well developed. The caudal fin, with a white band at the base, is scythe-shaped, with extended upper and lower lobes. A short black band can be seen behind the eyes and at the level of the fins on the caudal peduncle. The pectoral fins have a dark yellow edge. Measures 16 inches (40 centimeters) in length.

Whitecheek surgeonfish
Acanthurus nigricans

Tall, compressed, oval body. The caudal fin is scythe-shaped. Brownish, with yellow bands at the base of the dorsal and anal fins and the spines. The eyes and mouth are edged with white, and the caudal is white. Lives in lagoons and in the exposed zones of the reef down to a depth of 230 feet (70 meters). Measures up to 8.5 inches (21 centimeters) long.

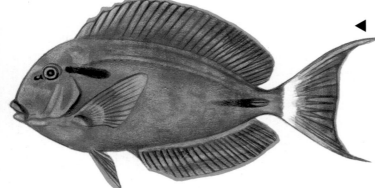

Convict tang
Acanthurus triostegus

Oval, compressed body. Dorsal and anal fins are rounded to the rear, and the caudal is truncated. The spine on the caudal peduncle is short and not clearly visible. Silvery gray with hints of yellow and six clearly visible dark vertical streaks, the first of which conceals the eye. Sometimes gathers in shoals when in search of the algae it feeds on. Measures up to 10 inches (25 centimeters) in length.

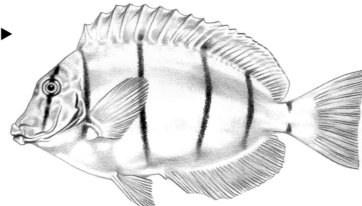

Lined surgeonfish
Acanthurus lineatus

Elongated, oval, and compressed body; rounded snout. Scythe-shaped pectoral fins. Crescent-shaped caudal with very extended lobes; caudal peduncle has a large spine. Eight to ten horizontal yellow and pale blue streaks on sides of body. Pale belly, yellow ventral fins with a black front edge. Territorial and aggressive, it is most frequently found in reefs exposed to the waves. Up to 16 inches (39 centimeters) long.

Orangespine unicornfish
Naso lituratus

Oval, compressed body, tall toward the front. The head is powerful, with a dorsal profile that forms a forty-five-degree angle. The snout is pointed; the mouth is small, lined with sharp teeth with rounded tips. On the sides of the peduncle are two bony plates, each bearing a sharp spine that curves forward. The caudal fin is semi-lunar, with pointed lobes and long filamentous rays. Yellowish brown, with an orange caudal peduncle, a light yellow spot between the eyes, and a yellowish orange dorsal fin, black at the base, with a white edge. Attains a length of 18 inches (45 centimeters).

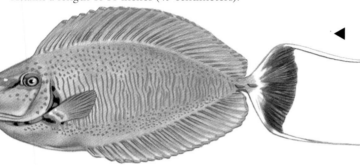

SCOMBRIDAE FAMILY

Dogtooth tuna
Gymnosarda unicolor

Body longer than other tuna species; dorsal and anal fins have white tips; color ranges from grayish-blue to greenish-blue on the back, while the sides and belly are silver. Breeds near reefs; feeds on small fish yet will attack larger fish near rocks. The size of schools varies; this fish ranges from an average of 3 feet (80 centimeters) to a maximum of 6 feet (180 centimeters).

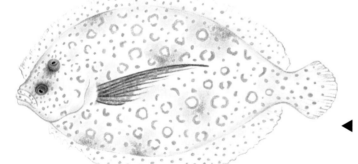

BALISTIDAE FAMILY

Redtoothed triggerfish
Odonus niger

Slightly oval body, with a pointed head. The mouth is terminal, and the lower jaw is more developed than the upper. Blue-black body; greenish head with bluish stripes leading from the mouth. The caudal fin is semilunar, the lobes well developed and quite long. This fish tends to gather in small groups, and grows to a length of 20 inches (50 centimeters).

Spotted unicornfish
Naso brevirostris

The most distinctive of the surgeonfish, easily recognized for its powerful oval body that terminates in a long beak, which in turn extends well beyond the snout. Two bony plates on the sides of the peduncle each bear a sharp spine. Rounded caudal fin. Ranges from grayish-blue to olive brown; lips are sometimes bluish. The tail features a pale band along the lower edge. This fish has gregarious habits, and attains a length of 20 inches (50 centimeters).

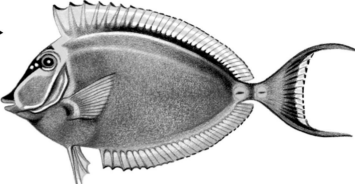

Vlaming's unicornfish (bignose unicornfish)
Naso vlamingii

Oval, elongated, and compressed body. The head has a slightly concave dorsal profile. Rounded snout, terminal mouth with protruding lips, and a very long dorsal fin, in which the first rays are filamentous. The ventral fins are small and thoracic. The caudal fin is truncated, with very long and filamentous lobes. The coloration is bluish with purple highlights, and a dark blue band over the eyes and the base of the tail. Can rapidly change color to very light or dark, depending upon its emotional state. These fish live in schools along the outer edge of the reef, and grow to be 18 inches (40 centimeters) in length.

BOTHIDAE FAMILY

Tropical flounder
Bothus mancus

Oval body, flattened and almost disk-shaped, with both eyes on the left side. Brownish gray, with large light blue ocelli. Males are distinguished by the very long rays of the pectoral fin. Lives on sandy seabeds in lagoons and along the reef, up to a depth of about 265 feet (80 meters). Up to 17 inches (42 centimeters) long.

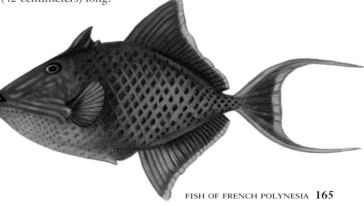

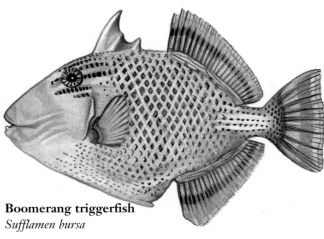

Boomerang triggerfish
Sufflamen bursa

Tall, compressed, lozenge-shaped body, with a conical head and pointed snout. Mouth at the end of the snout, with thick lips and protruding incisors. Pale in color. Between the rear of the eye and the pectoral fins are two yellowish brown streaks, the first of which resembles a boomerang in shape. A thin white streak runs from the mouth to the anal fin. Feeds on invertebrates living on the seabed. Measures up to 10 inches (24 centimeters) in length.

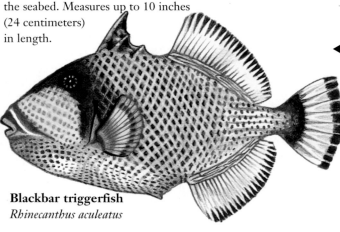

Blackbar triggerfish
Rhinecanthus aculeatus

Oval, compressed body. The conical head has a long, pointed snout. Front of the body and the belly are pale in color, while the rear part is dark. The mouth is edged with pale blue and yellow, and a stripe in the same colors runs as far as the pectoral fins. A black band edged with pale blue runs from the nape to the eyes. A series of oblique pale stripes runs along the sides, from the center to the belly. The caudal peduncle has three rows of small black spines. Reaches 12 inches (30 centimeters) in length.

OSTRACIIDAE FAMILY

Whitespotted boxfish
Ostracion meleagris

Robust body made of joined polygonal plates, also found at the mouth opening and the slots for the fins. Bluish, with yellow spots scattered around the body. Lives in lagoons and along the outer reef, to 100 feet (30 meters). Up to 7 inches (17.5 centimeters) long.

Yellowmargin triggerfish
Pseudobalistes flavimarginatus

The teeth are white and arranged in two rows above and one below. Base coloring is rather pale. There are black spots on the sides. The edges of the dorsal, anal, and caudal fins are yellowish. The scales at the base of the caudal are spiny. Measures up to 24 inches (60 centimeters) in length.

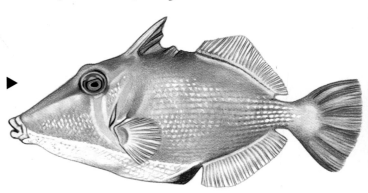

Titan triggerfish
Balistoides viridescens

Body shape is typical of the family. Mouth is terminal, and there is a deep groove between the eyes. Caudal peduncle, which is pale in color, has two to four horizontal rows of large tubercles. Greenish, with the fins black at the edges. A black band runs around the upper jaw. An aggressive species, especially during the mating season. Reaches 30 inches (75 centimeters) in length.

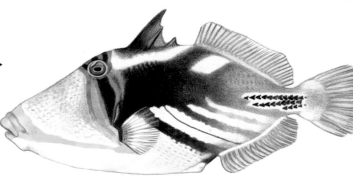

Halfmoon picassofish
Rhinecanthus lunula

Semirectangular body, tapering and compressed. The head has an almost triangular profile. Pale in color, with orange or brownish streaks along the sides. The caudal peduncle has an orange spot. Lives along the outer slopes of the reef, down to depths of 100 to 130 feet (30 to 40 meters). Measures up to 11 inches (28 centimeters) in length.

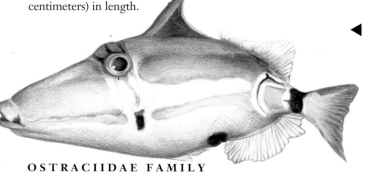

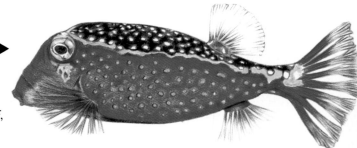

Yellow boxfish
Ostracion cubicus

Box-shaped and rectangular, with rounded angles and corners and no spines. Dorsal and anal fins are small but have powerful muscles that propel the fish. Ventral and caudal fins are more developed and act as rudders. Males are brilliant yellow with blue backs, females a uniform violet. Young individuals are yellow with black spots. Reaches 18 inches (45 centimeters) in length.

Longhorn cowfish
Lactoria cornuta

Boxlike, rigid polygonal body composed of bony plates welded together. Eyes in a dorsal position, protected by two large spiny appendages. Small mouth, with strong teeth for crushing the small invertebrates it captures after removing the sediments that cover them. Solitary, on sandy and detrital seabeds. Up to 18.5 inches (46 centimeters) long.

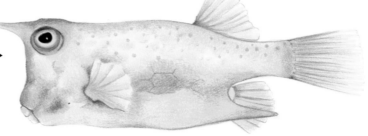

TETRAODONTIDAE FAMILY

Valentini's sharpnose puffer
Canthigaster valentini

Elongated, rounded body covered with a thick skin but no scales. Mouth is small and has teeth fused together to form a sort of beak. If frightened, it swells up. Territorial; lives in harems, males mating with numerous females. Prefers mixed seabeds. It is imitated by Paraluteres prionurus. Feeds on algae and invertebrates. Up to 4 inches (10 centimeters) long.

Black-spotted pufferfish (starry puffer)
Arothron stellatus

Elongated, globular body with an oval profile, covered with small spines. In young individuals this is rubbery, while it is more limp in adults. Mouth robust, with two large contiguous dental plates on each jaw. Typically spotted; in young individuals the belly has evident black stripes. Base of the pectoral fins is black. Swims by propelling itself with dorsal and anal fins. Not uncommon on the sandy bottoms of lagoons. Up to 36 inches (90 centimeters) long.

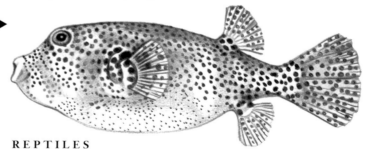

REPTILES

Green turtle
Chelonia mydas

Large turtle with a brown or olive green shell with four pairs of rib scales. Short, massive body. Found both in the open seas and close to coasts with bottoms overgrown with seaweed and underwater plants on which it feeds. It can lay eggs several times a year. Can reach a length of 42 inches (105 centimeters) and weigh up to 310 pounds (141 kilograms).

Hawksbill turtle
Eretmochelys imbricata

Commonly found close to coral reefs, identified by the black and yellow zigzag pattern of its scales, which also partially overlap. One of the most endangered turtle species, and protected by law. Feeds on sponges, mollusks, crustaceans, echinoderms, and seaweed. Can grow up to 36 inches (90 centimeters) long, with a weight of up to 265 pounds (120 kilograms).

Opposite: In the crystal clear waters off Bora Bora in the Society Islands, even snorkelers can admire a large number of marine species.

Text and Photographs: Kurt Amsler
Graphic Design: Maurizio Dondi
Dive Drawings: Cristina Franco
Maps: Maurizio Dondi
Marine Life Charts: Angelo Mojetta
Species Drawings: Monica Falcone and Lucia Mongioj
Translation: CTM, Milano
Production Editor: Kerrie Baldwin
Text Designer: Barbara Balch

KURT AMSLER has been awarded over one hundred prizes for his underwater photography, including the prestigious Sarra Prize, the Grand Master Prize at the Brighton Film Festival, and the Tridente d'Oro given by the Ustica Academy. He has published widely, including Abbeville's *The Caribbean Dive Guide.*

PHOTO CREDITS: All photographs are by Kurt Amsler, except of the following: *Philippe Bacchett:*1; 6 A, B, C, D; 18 B, D, E; 21 B, D; 30 A, B, D; 44 A, B, C, D; 52 A, B, C, D; 59 G; 62 A; 66 A, B, D, E, F; 68 B; 83 C; 84 A, B; 92 B; 101 C; 104 B; 106 A, C; 116 A, B, C; 120 B; 121 D; *White Star Archives:* 8 B, C; *Marcello Bertinetti / White Star Archives:* 21 C; *E.T. Archive:* 8 A; *NASA:* 19 C

SPECIAL THANKS:
Yves Lefevre of the Raie Manta Club, Rangiroa; Isabelle Amsler, my wife; Air France, Switzerland; Archipels Croisieres, Mooréa; Philippe Bacchett, Tahiti; Bernard Begliomini, Bathy's Club, Mooréa; Xavier Curvat, Plongee Marguises, Nuku Hiva; Nicolas Castel & Pierre Philippe Tricottet, Plongee-Eleutheraa, Tahiti; Philippe Cabral, Gauguin's Pearl Farm, Rangiroa; Arnaud Demietz and Ludovic Berne, Yacht Club, Tahiti; Christophe Lasherme, Videosub, Rangiroa; Nikon, Switzerland; Joel Orempuller, Tahiti; JWL-Aqualung, Germany and Switzerland; Raie Manta Club Team, Rangiroa; Yann Hubert; Anna and Jean-Jacques Gandy, Eric Leborgne and Didier Vogele, Jean-Marie, JoJo and Jean-Pierre; Thierry Sicard and Charly, Plongee Marquises, Nuku Hiva; Yannis Saint-Pe, Raie Manta Club, Tikehau; Tahiti Tourism, Paris & Papeete; Claude Sibani, Calypso Club, Bora Bora; John and Cynthia Sibani; Gregoire and Tamara Massonnet, Rangiroa; Pension Tuanake and Herenui, Rangiroa

First Edition
10 9 8 7 6 5 4 3 2 1

Library of Congress Cataloging-in-Publication Data

Amsler, Kurt.
    The French Polynesia dive guide / text and photography by Kurt Amsler.
        p.cm.
    ISBN 0-7892-0660-9 (alk. paper)
    1. Scuba diving—French Polynesia—Guidebooks. 2. French Polynesia Guidebooks. I. Title.
GV838.673.F84 A68 2000
797.2'3—dc21   00-029999